Visiting Your

ANCESTRAL
TOWN

Visiting Your

ANCESTRAL TOWN

A Yes You! Yes Now!® Book

Carolyn Schott

COLUMBIA-CAPSTONE

COLUMBIA-CAPSTONE

Yes You! Yes Now!®, with or without punctuation, is a registered trademark
of Columbia-Capstone

Published in the United States by Columbia-Capstone
Sammamish, Washington
www.columbia-capstone.com

Cover design by Arrowdesigns and TLC Graphics

ISBN-13: 978-0-9821148-4-1
ISBN-10: 0-9821148-4-2

Library of Congress Control Number: 2010929382

Library of Congress subject headings
Ancestry Travel
Family History
Family History Vacations
Genealogy
Genealogy Interview Questions
Genealogy Questionnaire
Genealogy Vacation
Travel
Travel Guidebook
Travel Planner

Dedicated to the Heaven's Hundred, the people who died at Maidan in Kyiv, giving their lives so my ancestral homeland of Ukraine might have a democratic government.

I wrote this second edition from December 2013 through February 2014, just as Ukraine's revolution was unfolding. Many days, I couldn't write as I watched the news of peaceful protesters being kidnapped, tortured, and shot by snipers, or as I kept vigil with the protesters (via live streaming from a TV camera set up at Maidan). The Maidan protesters won their battle for a new government, but not before many lives had been lost.

I also dedicate this to my parents, who instilled a love of family in me, and my genealogy mentor Dale Wahl who invited me on my first trip to ancestral towns in Ukraine.

Contents

Acknowledgements

Second edition
For the second edition, I'd like to thank my cousin, Justin Ehresman, and cousin-in-law, Meatra Keo, for letting me share their stories. I'm also indebted to Justin for reviewing a draft and giving me suggestions based on his own experience with genealogy and visiting ancestral towns.

I'm so thankful for my editors, Jennie Gulian and Kathy Burge, for everything they did to help make this book better. And publisher, Cyndie Tarr, has been a constant encouragement … and fun to work with besides!

Carolyn Schott
Seattle, Washington
April 2015

First edition
As I've been on my journey of researching my family history and traveling to my own ancestral towns, there have been many people who have inspired me, helped me, and made the journey special. Family members, genealogy colleagues, fellow travelers, guides, and new-found friends: you are too numerous to name, but I so appreciate each of you!

My special thanks to friends who have allowed me to share their stories and photos in this book: Gayla and Rich Aspenleiter, Valya and Milt Kramer, Elaine Morrison, Bob Schneider, Elli Wise. And I am also grateful to those who have guided me on my visits to ancestral villages in Ukraine: Serge Yelizarov and Peter on my first trip; Bob Schneider, Karolina Fromm, Inna Stryukova on my second trip.

I'd like to acknowledge my editor, Jennie Gulian, for her help. Jennie helped find the right words when I couldn't and gave me an objective perspective that I sometimes lost track of in the midst of writing. My publisher, Steve Tarr, has been of great encouragement and kept nudging me along when my writing progress slowed—thanks, Steve!

Chapter One

Why Visit Your Ancestral Town?

Visiting with the Kram family of Kassel (Komarivka), Ukraine

What's Your Reason?

Solving the family mystery no one ever talks about?
Wandering through cemeteries of crumbling, moss-covered
headstones? Finding out the truth about old family stories?
Discovering a connection between your life experiences and
those of your ancestors?

We each have our own set of reasons for visiting our ancestral
towns. You may have grown up listening to your parents' or

grandparents' stories of their childhoods. Or you may have been inspired by popular genealogy-based TV shows like *Who Do You Think You Are*, *Finding Your Roots*, or *Genealogy Roadshow*. As you research and get to know your ancestors across the centuries, it's natural to want to walk in their footsteps and see the places that influenced their lives.

Your own unique set of expectations for your travels into your family history will determine where to go and how to prepare.

Family memoirs and stories

Haven't we all heard our parents tell a story like, "Don't complain about walking to school, young lady. When I was your age, I'd milked the cows and fed the chickens before walking four miles to school."

But even as I rolled my eyes, my parents' and grandparents' stories gave me an intriguing glimpse into the world they grew up in that is so different from my world of the Internet and smartphones and Facebook. Their stories always made me want to see the places that they talked about.

My mother grew up in the town of Lehr, North Dakota, in the 1920s and '30s. Many of the memories of her youth grew fuzzier for her over time, but never the stories of the annual camp meetings her church held at the nearby Lehr Tabernacle. Even when she was in her eighties, her face would light up as she re-experienced the delight she and her friends had searching the straw floor for coins that had dropped from people's pockets. And then her stories would shift into her young adulthood, when she and her friends would walk into the prairie hills beyond the tabernacle, playing guitars and singing gospel songs, laughing, and of course, flirting with the young men.

Although I heard the stories of the camp meetings all my life and we visited my grandparents in Lehr throughout my childhood, I had never seen the tabernacle until I was an adult and took my mom to Lehr for the town's 100th anniversary. After a weekend of parades and church suppers, the final event of the celebration was a service in the tabernacle.

I was surprised to discover the tabernacle was so close to town, at the end of the street where my mother had lived and just across the county road. It was a surprise to see what a huge complex it was, with a separate kitchen building, dorms, washrooms, and a cabin for the visiting pastor, all in addition to the main tabernacle building. Seeing this for myself suddenly made my mom's stories make sense; how so many people could have come to the camp meetings from neighboring towns, and even the next state, and stayed for a whole week.

Seeing the familiar places opened the doors to new memories my mother had never shared before. "That field is where everyone would come and camp out. And I remember all of us sharing a cup to drink water from this pump," she explained, pointing to each location.

But my biggest revelation came during the service itself. My parents had faithfully taken me to church each Sunday when I was growing up. Even as a child I'd loved the music and singing and had never understood how my mother could dutifully stand

and hold the hymn book each service but never sing along. She appeared to be completely unmoved by the music.

But in the tabernacle on that Sunday morning in Lehr, the first song was an old gospel hymn, "When We All Get to Heaven." To my surprise, my mom sang out loudly and clearly, never even looking at the hymn book. After all these years, she still knew the words by heart.

When I asked her about it after the service, she said in her usual blunt fashion, "I've never liked those Presbyterian hymns, but I like the old evangelical gospel music!"

Sometimes the memories that are the most meaningful, the most important keys to understanding your family, lie below the surface and need the right trigger to come out. Sometimes you have to dig a little and ask some questions to learn more about your family. By visiting and experiencing her hometown through her eyes, I learned about my mother's love of music (at least, some types of music) that I'd never guessed.

Visiting towns of more distant ancestors

The visit to Lehr had a very personal connection for me because of my mother's stories. But I've also visited the towns of more distant ancestors, hoping for a feeling of connection by walking in their footsteps, by seeing the places where they once lived but chose to leave.

When I went to Hoffnungstal (Nadezhdivka in Ukrainian), an ethnic German village in Ukraine, I didn't expect much. From previous visitors, I'd learned the village had been destroyed. I would not get to see the house where my grandfather grew up or the church where he was confirmed. Even the cemetery had been destroyed, so I wouldn't even find the graves of my family members.

But even without those tangible family landmarks, I felt a sense of awe in seeing the valley as my great-great-grandparents, Peter and Katharina Schott, probably first saw it. They were among the earliest settlers, and when they arrived, there would have been few houses. As I stood on the cemetery hill, knowing that somewhere beneath my feet lay the bodies of those great-great-grandparents and dozens of other family members, I felt like I was seeing the lush, green valley with their eyes. I felt the sense of hope they must have felt that caused the village to be named Hoffnungstal (Hope Valley in German). I felt their sense of promise as they started a new life for their young family far away from their own parents and grandparents. And perhaps this same sense of hope and promise later caused my grandfather to leave there and come to America.

Traveling a road less traveled

Visiting an ancestral town can offer a unique travel experience away from typical tourist destinations and facilities. This gives you the opportunity to see a more remote location or connect with real people living there, rather than just tour guides and hotel clerks. (Unless, of course, your family came from a town that now happens to be a popular tourist destination. But that's not the case for most of us.)

A group of us from a genealogy organization I belong to traveled together to Ukraine to visit our ancestral towns. My friend Gayla was on a mission to photograph every house in her town of Neu Freudental (Marynove in Ukrainian). The rest of us were just killing time until she was done with her photography. So we wandered into the town's small grocery store, just one long counter and a few shelves, searching for ice cream on what had become a warm September day.

As we purchased our ice cream, I realized this might be my chance to get some extra batteries for my camera. We were directed to the next building, the town's general store, which we would never have guessed as there was no sign on the building. We spent a fascinating half hour poking through the odd selection of merchandise—socks lying next to nail scissors on the crowded counter; dresses hanging on the wall above the bags of cement for sale. But I bought my batteries and, at the same time, got a glimpse of the essential goods found in a general store in a small Ukrainian village.

Even more memorable was another friend's ancestral town, Kassel (Komarivka in Ukrainian). We stopped to see a local family, one of the few remaining that still had ethnic German connections. (Most of the ethnic Germans left these villages in the 1940s.) The family insisted we come in and have lunch with them.

Afraid we were straining their obviously limited financial resources, we insisted on sharing the food we'd brought along. In the one-room home, shared by three generations of this family, they pulled up the table next to the bed and brought in a bench from the yard outside to give us all a place to sit.

As we shared food and vodka, we also shared stories of our lives—ours in America and theirs in Ukraine. A daughter had moved back to this village to care for her elderly parents but was concerned about how hard it was to find work outside the cities. Then her face lit up as she mentioned her upcoming wedding. While their lives and homes were nothing like our own, their joys and cares were not that different.

Researching your family

You may want to visit an ancestral town to do more research on your family. Despite the growth of genealogy information on the Internet, there are many thousands, probably millions, of old documents *not* on the Internet that may be available locally. Talking to people in the town hall, church, or museum in your ancestral town or at a local archive that specializes in information about your town may bring insights that you would never get from sitting at your computer thousands of miles away. When my cousin visited an archive in the town of Landau, Germany, a local researcher's personal papers provided a breakthrough in his research.

Of course, the jackpot here is if you actually find some new information. I'll have to admit my research in my ancestral lands hasn't given me that "Eureka!" moment, though it has given me some important clues. And having the chance to handle 17th century documents in an archive or discuss the history of an area with a local expert has made for some interesting travel experiences.

A couple of years ago, I went to Germany. Through a German friend and by finding the archive's website, I discovered the archive that would help me find out information about my ancestors and learned I didn't need an appointment for a research visit. With the help of a European map website, I easily found the archive located on Wiesbaden's residential streets.

After putting everything but a pen and pad of paper into a locker, I presented myself to the collections desk where they helped me request records through their computer system. Then I stationed myself at a table until one of the archive workers wheeled up a cart stacked with documents, delivering them from the depths of wherever they are kept to me and other waiting researchers.

Although my research that day mostly helped me find where my ancestors weren't, I was a bit in awe at being able to walk in off the street and handle documents from the 1600s, some with the original wax seal still barely attached. I read through tax lists and crop lists (which showed lists of village residents). I even found an interesting document in which a Schott widow begged the local count to excuse her from paying taxes because, she argued, her husband had worked hard in the count's service yet never made a penny. She even scolded the count a bit. I was sorry I couldn't find a relationship to me—she sounded spunky and interesting, and I would have loved to claim her as a many-times great-grandmother.

And in the end, this research trip did pay off. Although I left disappointed, it did make me question if I had the right village since none of my family names showed up in the records I'd looked at. Sure enough, several years later, I found out my family actually had lived in a different town with a similar name.

Although the research only helped in a roundabout way, the experience was worthwhile. Even an apparent dead end can be part of the adventure.

◆　◆　◆

What Will I Experience in My Ancestral Town?

Will you meet a long-lost relative? Or find the grave of the grandparent you've heard stories about? Absorb a new culture in a land where your family once lived? Or experience the disappointment of discovering your ancestral town has been paved over and there is no trace of your family history?

Your experience in your ancestral town will depend on a combination of your expectations, your preparation, and a little luck. Do as much planning as you have time for, then be willing to experience whatever unfolds. While that has sometimes led to disappointments for me, more often it has led to serendipitous, interesting encounters I could never have orchestrated.

Planning a little or a lot

On my first trip to Germany, I was content just to be in the same country where my ancestors had lived. I had no idea what town they'd come from and didn't care. Although I didn't speak enough German at the time to understand what was being said, the cadence of the language was familiar to my ears from hearing it as a child and gave me a sense of familiarity. The smell of the sausage and various "dough dishes" (dumplings, *spätzle*) weren't exactly the same as my mother had cooked but were familiar enough that I dived into everything on my plate while my fellow travelers were still timidly poking at their food. Just the realization that the surroundings felt comfortable, even though I'd traveled thousands of miles to a different culture, was enough to make that trip a success for me.

On a later trip, I'd done more research and knew some of the towns where my ancestors had lived. But I still didn't do much more preparation than finding the location on the map. Most of these villages are small, so once I located them and drove through once, there wasn't much more to see. I visited cemeteries, but most cemeteries in Germany are recycled every 30 years, so I couldn't find any graves of my ancestors (who had all left Germany by the early 1800s). I looked at the locked churches and even bought a pastry in one local bakery. But I left without interacting with anyone. It was interesting, but not an especially meaningful visit for me.

More recently, I visited the town of Ober-Gleen, Germany. For this trip, I did quite a bit of preparation, including making plans to spend the day with the owner of a small art gallery in the town. Someone from the town hall, which I'd contacted via their website, had put me in touch with him because he had an interest in local history. I spent a fabulous day with Herr Bloemers, who showed me around the museum in the neighboring town, shared local history, and gave me some insights into why my ancestor might have left. He had a key to the church, so I got to tour that and even saw the baptismal font where my ancestors were probably baptized. I stayed overnight at a B&B in the next town and ate some of the best *spätzle* of my life. We had afternoon cake and coffee in the courtyard of his small art gallery and he told me lively stories about some of his experiences working all over the world for a luxury hotel chain.

It was a fabulous day with an interesting guide and new insights into my ancestors—all because I did a little planning.

Serendipitous experiences

On a trip to Ukraine, I thought I'd prepared thoroughly. I had a map of the village from the time period my ancestors had lived there. I highlighted all the homes with family names and figured out how each related to my family (some were the houses of cousins rather than my direct line).

But the most interesting part of this visit had nothing to do with my planning. It came from meeting Nadia, the vice principal of the school. She showed a group of us around the school (interrupting the classes to the children's delight and the teachers' irritation) and told us its history, and then showed us around the village and to some of the homes I'd highlighted on my map. From hearing the school's history, I realized my great-grandparents had probably gone to school in this very building. Nadia insisted I sit in one of the desks, just like my great-grandparents had.

On a trip to Germany, I'd arranged to meet Friedrich, a distant cousin. He was such a distant cousin that, when I first e-mailed him, I wasn't even sure how we were related. I only knew there was a connection because my friend and fellow researcher Dale had assured me of it.

Friedrich immediately invited me to stay with him and his wife. This felt a bit odd since I didn't know them at all. But since Dale knew them, I figured it would be okay for one night at least. Then I would continue on with my travel plans, which mostly involved visiting tourist sites—castles and museums.

Friedrich and Ute were so welcoming that I ended up staying with them for three nights instead of just one. They immediately invited me back the following weekend for a family birthday celebration and again later that month to visit a local wine festival. Then they said, "So what other relatives are you planning to visit?"

I hadn't known others even existed. Friedrich insisted on contacting relatives all over Germany to make plans for me to visit them. Instead of the simple tourist month I'd planned, I ended up meeting many new relatives, several of whom I still regularly communicate with 17 years later. I missed some of the tour book sights I'd planned on visiting but saw others through the eyes of a local, who also happened to be a distant cousin.

I could never have planned for nor predicted this experience. The personal connections I made gave much more meaning to my search for my family history. The search became more about connecting with people rather than just places.

Disappointments

Of course, travel also brings uncertainty. There are missed connections or bad weather or incorrect information or bad timing. Any of these may cause you to miss something you'd hoped to see. As a regular tourist, that can be frustrating. But on a once-in-a-lifetime trip to visit an ancestral town, these disappointments may feel devastating. Fortunately, the types of problems that can completely ruin a trip are rare.

Sometimes disappointment comes when a place that should be meaningful and full of family history has changed too much. I look at the now lonely hillside in North Dakota where my grandfather's farm once stood and where my father grew up. Many buildings are gone, so I have a hard time visualizing the big white house built by my father's uncle, the farmyard bustling with chickens, or the large red barn that all have been described to me.

Where was the barn in relation to the house? And how did my parents manage to "borrow" my grandfather's car out of the barn late at night, pushing it down the hill without starting it (which might wake him up) to get it down to the road? Then, how did they manage the process in reverse as my dad brought my mom home from their date?

I've always loved that story because it shows a mischievous side of my parents in their youth that I never saw in them. But the current bare hillside doesn't help me visualize it any better than if I'd just stayed home in Seattle.

What will it be like to visit an ancestral town?

Every trip and set of experiences is unique. Hopefully your trip will avoid the disappointing moments and allow you to experience something that you would never have expected while sitting at home in front of your computer planning your trip.

Chapter Two

Discovering Your Ancestral Town

Visiting my ancestral town of Boginia, Poland

Getting Started

The first step in visiting a place where your family has roots is simply to discover where your ancestors came from, the country or town where they were born, had children, lived, and died. That may be easy and common knowledge in your family. But in most cases, it requires doing some research. Knowing basic genealogical research methods is crucial to truly discovering your family roots.

Even if you think you already know where your roots are, doing the research might lead to some surprises. After growing up firm in the knowledge that my family was German (my parents spoke German, my mother cooked German food), it was a big surprise when I discovered a book that showed my grandparents had been born in "South Russia." This seeming contradiction is actually what spurred my interest in finding out more and diving headfirst into learning about my family history.

The genealogy guidance in this book will feature the areas I have the most experience researching in—the United States, Germany, and Eastern Europe. But wherever your family roots are, genealogy principles and many of the resources are the same wherever your family search leads you.

What do you already know?

The best place to start is with what you already know about your family. Of course, some family situations are complicated. You may not know much because there may be missing links and family mysteries that were never talked about. Solving these mysteries may be the reason you're starting this research in the first place.

But even if your knowledge is limited, the best foundation to build on is the family information you already know. Who are your parents? Your siblings? Your grandparents, aunts and uncles, and cousins? Do you know when and where they were born or married or died?

Write it all down and document how you know this information (more about documenting sources a little bit later).

Even if there are lots of gaps in your information, this gives you a foundation to build on as you start your journey into family history.

Choosing genealogy software

As you build up your collection of genealogy data, you'll need a way to keep track of it all. This used to be simple—the two choices were paper and a limited set of PC- or Mac-based software programs. Now the selection is dizzying and includes online options and apps for tablets and smartphones. To wade through all the choices, consider the following:

- Determine the features you need. I'd suggest making a list of three to five features most important to you as you compare your options.
- Considerations include: How easily does the software allow you to enter family information? Do you want it to create a family history book or website? Does it allow you to easily add media files (photos, videos, etc.) to individuals in your tree and tag the source of the information? Does it provide flexible options to report on your family data (tree format, report format, etc.)? Does it track genealogy DNA results?
- Determine the device(s) you will use most often for your genealogy. They may include your laptop, tablet, or smartphone. Does the software synch or provide access where you need it to?

These sources may help you identify your software options:

- Top Ten Reviews does an annual comparison of the top software programs for PCs and Macs: http://software.toptenreviews.com/reference-lifestyles.

- Cyndi's List provides links for mobile device options, genealogy software, and online genealogy software, but it doesn't include comparisons of the different options: (www.cyndislist.com/mobile, www.cyndislist.com/software/genealogy, www.cyndislist.com/software/online-family-trees).

- Dick Eastman is an authoritative voice on genealogy technology who blogs about software and genealogy apps for tablets and smartphones at: http://blog.eogn.com/category/software.

I would be cautious about using an online family tree tool as your only genealogy database. Some sites that offer this service charge a subscription fee. Do you want to be trapped forever into subscribing because all of your precious genealogy data is there? What if the site crashes or goes out of business? (Admittedly, this is unlikely with some of the largest genealogy providers but it's still something to keep in mind.)

On the other hand, it can also be dangerous for your only genealogy database to be on your laptop, as that can crash or be stolen. Backing up your data is vital, as well as storing your backup drive separately from your computer to prevent both from being stolen. Having your data online, in addition to on your laptop, or backing up your data in the cloud (Internet) is crucial for protecting the valuable family data on your laptop.

Personally, I have my main genealogy database (using Family Tree Maker software) on my laptop, the device that is most comfortable for me to use to enter data and to scan and attach photos and documents. I also have my family tree loaded to an online website (the Black Sea German Research site, which is free and focused on my specific area of research). This makes it easy for me to connect with other researchers and to access my genealogy information using my Droid smartphone wherever I am.

The only slight disadvantage to my approach is when I'm talking with a newly discovered relative, I can't immediately enter their data using my ever-present smartphone. Even though I've started to look into getting an app for my smartphone, I also recognize that wrestling with software may not be the best method for jotting down data during an interview. ("Wait, where was your grandfather born again? Just a minute, let me tab over to that field. His father? Wait, wait, I need to click on a different page. Just a sec, my connection seems to be slow right now.")

I've found that recording a conversation or jotting down notes on my phone's notes app or even on paper has actually worked quite well for me even without a genealogy app on my smartphone.

What does your family know?

Now it's time to expand your research by interviewing your family members—parents, grandparents, aunts, uncles, cousins.

Ask everybody. Ask anyone who will sit still for a moment to tell you what they know or have heard about your family.

Don't be shy. Call Great-Aunt Martha even if no one in the family has spoken with her in a decade. In fact, *especially* call Great-Aunt Martha and any other older relatives. They often have a fount of knowledge, including family legends, stories of family black sheep, and little tidbits of information that you will never be able to find in any official source such as vital records or church records.

I spent last Christmas in my dad's hometown. My cousin invited an older couple over for coffee so I could talk with Jim about the times he worked for my grandfather as a teen, and also find out what he knew about my dad and uncle's local business ventures in the 1940s.

Jim laughed when he got the invitation. "We always used to want to talk with the old people about how things used to be. And now I am the old people!" But he had several anecdotes about my grandfather hiring him and other teens to clear rocks from the fields and paying them in cigarettes. He knew some great background information about all the car dealerships in the area, which helped me better understand my dad and uncle starting a new car dealership in their hometown of Kulm, North Dakota, and he even remembered some of my dad's customers.

And (not to be morbid) don't wait to interview your older relatives. I'll always regret not talking with my Aunt Edna, who was interested in our family history and knew all sorts of family stories from her mother, my grandmother, who died when I was only 3 years old. Aunt Edna was always such a ball of energy; I could never imagine a time she wouldn't be around. She lived nearby so it was easy to put it off thinking, "Oh, I can easily run over there one day and ask her a few questions." But before I got around to it, Aunt Edna died suddenly of a heart attack at age 77.

Don't wait.

Interviewing and using family legends to further your research

If your family member is comfortable with this, record your interview as that will let you focus on the conversation, rather than concentrate on taking notes or fumbling with your genealogy software. Ideally, record your conversation so it can be stored digitally rather than on cassette because tape is fragile and difficult to replay as these become obsolete. I often use a digital voice recorder, but video or your smartphone will also work.

If the person you are interviewing is relaxed and feels like they're just having a conversation with you, they're much more likely to remember interesting details than if they feel pressured by you recording each detail in your computer or smartphone. A strict interview format may make them try so hard to answer your questions that they actually won't remember as much as if they'd just been free to reminisce.

Some people will be naturals—you can ask a couple of open-ended questions, and they'll eagerly spill out hours of interesting family information and memories. But others will need a bit more prompting. It's good to come prepared with a list of questions and topics you want to cover. See the Appendix for a list of some questions you might ask.

When you talk to family members, ask them what they know or remember about their parents, aunts and uncles, and grandparents. Ask them if they know the dates they were born, married, or died. Ask them where they lived, when they moved, and what they did for a living. Ask them if they have any photos, as these can provide useful clues about family connections. Armed only with a formal family photo belonging to her grand-aunt and the family legend that in her great-grandfather's family, "all the girls stayed in Sweden and all the boys came to America," a friend of mine did a letter writing campaign to all the members of the Lilja family in a town in Nebraska to identify the connections between the Lilja family in the photo and her Peterson family.

Ask your family members if they know if anyone else in the family has ever done genealogy research in the past. My Netz family research started out with an extensive foundation because a distant aunt had once done research and sent it to my cousin, who was more than willing to get rid of it by giving it to me when I asked.

Encourage them to talk about unproven family legends and rumors. Not only will these help you get to know your ancestors as real people, rather than just as names and dates, but these legends can also give you important clues that will actually help your research.

Two family legends helped me find my grandfather's name on a ship's passenger list. One rumor, which was voiced in our family over and over again, was that my grandfather had been a stowaway on a ship to the U.S. The second rumor, the source of which I don't remember, was that my grandfather had used his married brother-in-law's passport to come to the U.S. because it allowed him to escape military conscription in Russia.

There were holes in both of these stories. About three-fourths of the German-Russian researchers I know have family stories about their immigrant ancestors being stowaways, and I don't think any of them have proven to be true. And although my grandfather's brother-in-law was married, that wouldn't necessarily have exempted him from military service in early 1900s Russia, so using the brother-in-law's passport would not have helped my grandfather avoid military conscription. Also, the U.S. didn't require a passport to enter in 1905 when my grandfather arrived.

So I set out to find his passenger list and disprove the prevalent stowaway rumor. And yet, I couldn't find it anywhere. Peter Schott was not on any passenger list index I could find. The shipping line that he referenced on his Declaration of Intent (one step in the process of becoming a citizen) had a number of ships arriving in the U.S., but none seemed to have arrived in the main port of New York at the right time to match when he got to North Dakota. I started to wonder if he'd purposely provided misleading information and maybe the stowaway legend was true after all.

On a whim, I decided to look for his brother-in-law, Jakob Schuldheisz. I knew Jakob came to the U.S., so I expected to find him in the passenger list index and didn't expect that would help my search for my grandfather Peter. Sure enough, I found Jakob on the index right away. Oddly, it showed him arriving on a ship that was earlier than when I knew he had immigrated. But it was exactly the same time that my grandfather had arrived. I decided to check it out.

The microfilm of the passenger list for this ship from Bremen to Baltimore simultaneously answered my question and created a new one that I haven't solved to this day. In different writing than the original passenger list, the name Schuldheisz had been converted to Schott by scratching out the *heisz*, turning the *u* to an *o*, and crossing the *ld* to make it look like *tt*. Jakob had been scratched out and changed to Peter, and his contacts in the U.S. had been changed from "friends Fred and Christ Schott in North Dakota" to "bro Fred and Christ Schott in North Dakota." It clearly looked like Jakob Schuldheisz had originally been written then later changed to Peter Schott. This was my grandfather's passenger list entry.

Without knowing the rumor about the passport, I would never have found Peter Schott on a passenger index as Jakob Schuldheisz and would never have proven that my grandfather wasn't a stowaway. At the same time, it creates a mystery I may never solve. Why did my grandfather use his brother-in-law's name on the passenger list? (Even if he used Jakob's passport to get out of Russia, surely there wouldn't have been any danger of getting caught by the Russian government when he was boarding the ship in Germany.) When and why did the passenger list get corrected? Did he accidentally give himself away that his name wasn't Jakob, which forced it to be corrected? Or did he simply want to set the record straight? And was the loan of the passport the reason that Jakob and family didn't come to the U.S. for another 6 years? (I can't imagine how difficult it must have been to convince the Russian government in 1905, "Woops, I lost my passport and need a new one.")

I may never know the answers to these questions, unless I can find someone who knows another family legend.

◆ ◆ ◆

Documenting Your Research

Every fact you put into your family tree should be documented with the source of the information. Yes, I really mean *every* one.

When you start your research, it's easy to think, "Oh, those are my cousins; I know I got all that information from Uncle Joe." Or, "This book on Kilkenny has so much information; I'll know that anything I have recorded about Kilkenny came from this book."

But as you expand your research into vital records and church records and other researchers' family trees, you'll start to discover conflicting information. Did my Schott family come from Ludwigsburg, Germany (as listed in a book of family origin data

25

that was compiled 130 years after the family arrived in Russia) or in Osthofen, Germany (as listed in the Osthofen church records)? Were my Billigmeier great-great-great-grandparents married in 1811 (information sent to me by one researcher), 1814 (sent to me by another researcher), or 1812 (the Gräfenhousen, Germany, church records)?

Knowing your sources enables you to sort out the data that is most likely to be correct when you have conflicting data. Having bad data can lead you astray in your genealogy ... and lead you to the wrong place if you're planning a trip to visit an ancestral town. If you don't know your sources, it's impossible to figure out which piece of conflicting information is more reliable.

A few tips in documenting your sources include:

- Document everything, even facts you personally know. The source on my parents' birth dates is: "Carolyn Schott, personal knowledge" since I know these because we celebrated them each year.

- Document even informal conversations with relatives or other researchers that provide family data. Include their name and the date of the conversation, e-mail message, Christmas card, etc. The source in my family tree for several recent babies in the family is "Per birth announcement by [mom's name] on Facebook [date]."

- Make copies (digital or paper) of documents (such as census records or church records) in which you find information, in addition to noting the reference information (e.g., page number). Most genealogy software allows you to attach images to individuals, which you can use to attach JPGs or PDFs of the documentation as well as photos. Sometimes, as you learn more about your family, there will be clues in the original document that you didn't notice at first that will help you later.

- Document where you've looked for information, even if you don't find anything. This will prevent you from covering the same ground over again later. I can't tell you how many times I've looked at an ancestor in my family tree and thought, "I should really go find her birth date," only to realize when I'm looking at the relevant church record that I've already looked at it multiple times before—and it still doesn't have the piece of information I'm looking for. I need to expand my research to new sources.

- Make a note of and document even the crazy family stories. While they may not be accurate, they can be great clues to help you find the real facts. (Just make sure you don't record them as fact until you verify that the crazy story really happened.)

When evaluating sources of conflicting data to determine which source is most reliable, some of the factors to consider include:

- Is the source of your information an original record (or an actual image of the original)? Or is it a derivative? Derivative sources include transcriptions, translations, or data extracted from original records. These processes leave room for error, so they are less reliable.

- Did the person supplying the information have first-hand knowledge of the event? A parent's information on the birth date of a child is more likely to be correct than a distant relative reporting on the birth.

- How near in time to the event was it recorded? A marriage recorded in a town's church records (which would usually happen at the same time as the actual event) is more reliable than a marriage date shown in a census that was recorded 40 years later.

- Are there any biases or external conditions that would affect the accuracy of the information? Children are frequently listed on ship passenger lists as younger than they actually were so they could pay a lower fare. For my German Russians, a valuable source of family data is the forms filled out by families in the 1940s when they were being repatriated from Russia to Germany and had to prove their German ethnicity by documenting several generations of ancestors. But since they were being forced to abandon their homes and most of their possessions, it's highly likely they were distressed enough not to fill out every date exactly correctly.

All of this may sound complicated, but it's really just common sense. Write down where you got your information so you can figure out what is most likely to be accurate—an official record or the unreliable memory of an elderly relative recalling events that happened 80 years before.

◆ ◆ ◆

Expanding Your Research

In parallel with talking to your family members, you'll probably want to dive into more resources to start expanding your research. Some of these include:

- **Online sources:** There has been an explosion in the last five to ten years of genealogy information online, as well as numerous websites devoted to this popular hobby. Online sources of information can include original records (images or extracts of the data in the records), family trees that other researchers have compiled, and numerous sites that specialize in specific types of records or types of research.

- **Vital records:** These are official civil records such as birth certificates, marriage licenses, and death certificates. Availability of these varies in each country. In the U.S., they are generally available at the state level. Some countries have national-level civil registration. Cyndi's List or an Internet search will help you find the links to the state or national vital records offices.

- **Church records:** These records include births, marriages, deaths, confirmation records (useful for estimating a birth date since confirmation usually happened at about age 14), and family books. Church records often have the most complete record of family events. In times when travel was difficult, civil registration was often deferred or ignored, while births, marriages, and deaths were immediately recorded at the local church. The best way to find these records is usually through the Family History Library (vast source of genealogical data based in Salt Lake City) and through church archives. It's fun to think that seeing the local church records and finding a new discovery will be part of your visit to an ancestral town. But in many (probably most cases) these records have been consolidated into a central church archive, which is usually located in a larger city.

- **Census records:** These records vary in format and content but usually list all members of the family and their ages. They often list where the family came from (at least the country or state), and later U.S. censuses show country of birth, occupation, and other interesting information. Russian censuses also have helped me find out key information about where a family lived in a village and previous villages where they lived that I hadn't known about.

- **Immigration records:** These types of records may include ships' lists, passport lists, etc. The format and content of each type of record varies, but immigration records are helpful in researching movement from one location to another. These usually include all family members and show the place where the family was planning to move.

Be systematic in your approach

As you expand your research efforts, it's best to be systematic in your approach. Start from the information you know and build on that as you work backward in time, discovering new ancestors generation by generation.

Don't make the mistake of generically researching anyone with your family name or researching a famous person with your name, assuming you're somehow related and that your family is from the same places they're from.

For example, I've tracked each birth and marriage of my Schott family ancestors to document their lives in North Dakota, and then prior to that in the German villages in the Black Sea area of Ukraine, and then back to their village in Rheinland/Pfalz, and before that to Hessen. I've resisted the temptation to research Marge Schott, the now deceased, loud-mouthed former owner of the Cincinnati Reds baseball team; Ben Schott, best-selling author; Ernest Schott, my high school librarian; the owners of Schott Music (a multinational music publishing company founded in 1770); or the owners of Schott Glass Corporation (a multinational company focused on glass technology with $2.7 billion in annual sales). All of these are more famous (well, except maybe my high school librarian) than my own Schott family line. But in researching my own line of Schotts back to the 1600s, I have never found a connection with any of these other Schott families. If I'd researched their families, or visited places where those Schotts are from, I would have wasted my time and my travel dollars.

♦   ♦   ♦

Using Online Resources

Searching online is the best first step to discover the records that are available or the genealogy data that someone else has already found about your family. And it's certainly more convenient (though maybe not as much fun) as a trip to an archive to dig through musty records on your own. There are basically two types of records you'll find online. The first is original sources and the second is other people's research and family trees.

Original sources

Original sources that are online may include census lists, church records, military records, vital records, etc. In some cases, the actual image of the record will be online. These online images are nirvana to a researcher since the absolute best way to ensure that you are capturing accurate information is by looking at a source yourself.

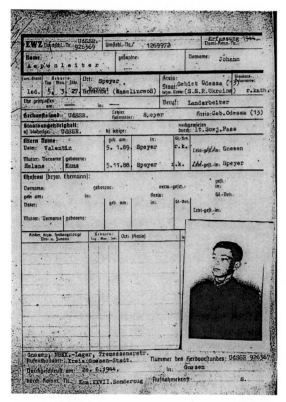

Image of an original EWZ (Einwanderungzentralstelle or Central Immigration Control Department) record for Johann Aspenleiter (the distant cousin of a friend of mine), showing his mother as Helene Kunz, who was the first wife of Valentin Aspenleiter.

Record obtained from the U.S. National Archives and Records Administration.

An extract of a record will generally include all relevant data from the image of the record. For example, an extract of a church marriage record would include the marriage date, bride and groom's names, and often additional information such as the fathers of the bride and groom or their town of origin. Often extracts are translated into English.

While it's still best to find and look at the actual record yourself to ensure the data has been extracted correctly, I often rely on extracts depending on how accessible the actual record is and how close the relationship of the ancestor. (For a direct ancestor, I always view the original source for verification. For data on a sixth cousin five times removed, I might be willing to be lazy and accept the information in an extract.)

Extract of the EWZ record for Johann Aspenleiter from the Black Sea German Database. This extract is of a different EWZ record than the previous illustration and shows Rosa Krieger, Valentin Aspenleiter's second wife, as the mother of Johann Aspenleiter. This is a great example of why it is important to check original sources and multiple sources.

Courtesy of the Black Sea German Research Community, www.blackseagr.org.

An index of a record is usually just a finding aid, showing you a key piece of information (such as the groom's name) and the page number of the record. To find all the juicy data, you still need to look at the actual record or an extract of the record.

Index listing for Johann Aspenleiter, providing a pointer to the microfilm with the original image and more information.
Courtesy of the Odessa3 website, www.odessa3.org.

Online family trees

The second type of online resource is family trees that others have already researched. These can be an incredibly valuable source of information. These can be an incredibly terrible source of information. Yes, I really meant to say they're both valuable and terrible.

Online family trees are valuable because it makes sense to share knowledge and this source can save you from having to retrace research steps completed by another researcher. But there are many pitfalls to be aware of. A couple of these are:

- Not everyone who posts their family trees is a diligent researcher who verifies their sources. Sadly, many people grab information from any source and record it as fact, without ever verifying if it's actually true. I'd hate to visit what I thought was an ancestral town and later find out it is completely unconnected with my family—simply because I trusted a researcher who didn't reliably check their sources.

- Honest mistakes can be perpetuated. For many years, I thought one of my 3X-great-grandmothers was Rosina Hensel, first wife of Christian Hinz, simply because I didn't check the dates closely enough to realize my direct ancestor was a child of Christian and his second wife, Wilhelmine Mueller. An honest mistake of mine in working with the church records. When I found it, I fixed it in my family tree. But anyone who looked at my data before I fixed this mistake has the incorrect data ... and I have no way to tell them that it's been changed.

When you use information from someone else's family tree posted online, always check to see if they have a source listed, and then look at that original source to verify the information.

In one online family tree from a researcher I don't know, my grandfather's birthplace is listed as Hoffnungstal, South Russia, and shows a source (his WWI draft registration). But when I looked at his draft registration record, nowhere did it actually show his birthplace. In this case, I had another source that verified that information. But if that researcher had shown my grandfather's birthplace in an incorrect town, and if I accepted the source without checking, I would have the wrong information about my ancestral town. My search would be at a dead end, unable to find previous generations of my ancestors because I'd be looking in the wrong town.

Information in a family tree without a verified source is a good clue, but is not reliable data. Never take information from an online source without verifying it for yourself.

If you do use information from an online family tree, be sure to do the following:

- Note the researcher and their family tree as one of your sources. This is partly good documentation of your research and partly common courtesy to acknowledge someone else's hard work.

- Never use a photo or document attached to the family tree (*especially* if you're planning to publish it in a family history book or website) without getting the permission of the owner. Not only is this common courtesy, but of course it's also important to follow copyright law. (If you have questions on copyright law in the U.S., see www.copyright.gov. If you have questions on copyright law in Canada, see http://laws-lois.justice.gc.ca/eng/acts/C-42/.)

Online genealogy sources

There are more online sources of genealogy information than I can possibly cover in this book, and new ones pop up every day. So I'll just include a sampling of the most important ones.

Family Search (www.familysearch.org)

This is a free site, associated with the Family History Library (FHL), the "mother ship" of all genealogical knowledge. The FHL has been microfilming genealogy records for more than 70 years. At the beginning of 2014, it had about 2.4 million rolls of microfilm in its storage site in Utah. There is an enormous effort underway, which includes thousands of volunteers, to index, extract, and digitize this vast collection of genealogical data.

The FHL's digitized, online data spans the globe. As of 2014, the largest number of online collections are for the U.S. and continental Europe. There are also a large number of collections for the Caribbean, Central and South America; the U.K. and Ireland; Canada; and Mexico. There are also a number of collections digitized for Asia and the Middle East; Africa; Australia and New Zealand; and the Pacific Islands. (Keep in mind that the FHL's digitized online data is only the tip of the iceberg. Many of the records I'll describe in the "Moving Beyond Online Resources" section can be found on microfilm in the FHL, available through its local branches—also called Family History Centers—even though they're not digitized and online.)

The one caution I have in using this extracted data is that if you find one type of information digitized for a town, don't assume that's all there is and skip checking the microfilm records that aren't online. I found marriage and birth information for my Schott family in the online records for Ober-Gleen, Germany. But the more complete microfilm version of these church records also includes death information that hasn't been digitized yet and which provided some key information on my family. If I'd assumed everything for the town was online, I would have missed some important family history.

Family Search also includes a large number of user-submitted genealogy family trees—including the Ancestral File, the Pedigree Resource File, and much of the International Genealogical Index (IGI). Again, these are great resources, but don't use the information found there without checking for documented sources and verifying those sources with your own eyes.

Family Search also has some great research guides by ethnicity (e.g., German or Irish or Jewish ancestry) or specific topics (e.g., Finding Immigrant Ancestors).

Ancestry (www.ancestry.com)

This is a fee-based subscription service that provides access to an extensive set of records online. In 2013, it was estimated to have more than 11 million historical records. These include census and voter lists; birth, marriage, and death records; obituaries; military information; passenger lists; land records; tax lists; church and school directories; maps and gazetteers; and more. Is your head spinning yet? This can be the Mecca of genealogy information, but beware. Ancestry, while a great service, is much stronger in their U.S., Canadian, and U.K. and Ireland collections than in any other part of the world. If your ancestors have spent the last few hundred years in any of these places, Ancestry will be of great value to you. If, like me, your ancestors were mostly living in other places, you will need to expand your horizons to other sources of information.

In addition to the original documents that are online for subscribers to view, Ancestry also has an extensive set of public member trees that fellow researchers have contributed. These are great sources of information. But as I said previously, use these cautiously. Check for sources and verify any that are noted.

Ancestry has separate websites for the U.S., U.K., Canada, Germany, Italy, Australia, France, and Sweden. Generally you have the option to either subscribe to the country you're in or, at a higher price, to worldwide membership so you can access all available records. As an alternative, many libraries (including Family History Centers and other genealogy organization libraries) have a worldwide subscription that you can access on the library's computers.

Cyndi's List (www.cyndislist.com)

Cyndi's List, a volunteer effort by Cyndi Howell, is the ultimate set of links one can ever hope to find for genealogy. While Cyndi's List doesn't have actual records available, it does provide links to anything and everything genealogical. Looking for how to get started? Looking for genealogy blogs? Looking for vital records for your Cajun ancestors? Trying to figure out an unusual calendar entry in a record? Looking for information on royalty or genealogy software or creating a family history book or hiring a professional researcher? Cyndi's List has got you covered.

Find a Grave (www.findagrave.com)

Find a Grave is a volunteer-based site that catalogs gravestones and cemeteries. With a database of 111 million grave records in more than 400,000 cemeteries in more than 200 countries (as of 2014), it is an incredible source to help find your ancestors' last resting place and any information from their headstones. Some entries include photos of the headstones.

USGenWeb (usgenweb.org) and RootsWeb (www.rootsweb.ancestry.com)

USGenWeb and RootsWeb are websites of free genealogical information for the U.S., maintained by volunteers. Since the records included are at the discretion (or whim) of the volunteers, the types of records you'll find might seem a bit random. But these are still great places to find vital records, cemetery transcriptions, county histories, maps, etc., from people who really know their local areas. The websites also include online forums, where you can post questions and interact with other researchers. These forums are searchable and the questions and answers are archived, which allows you to connect with researchers who may have posted a question months previously. I solved one family mystery because another researcher, who had the parts of the genealogical puzzle I lacked, found my inquiry on a forum a year after I posted it.

USGenWeb is organized primarily at the state level, while RootsWeb is more focused on county-specific records.

WorldGenWeb (www.worldgenweb.org)

WorldGenWeb is also run by volunteers and includes free genealogical information or links to research resources for numerous countries around the world. The site also includes good historical background that may help you better understand what records to look for.

Ellis Island (www.ellisisland.org), Castle Garden (www.castlegarden.org), German Roots (www.germanroots.com/passengers.html), and Steve Morse's site (www.stevemorse.org)

When you think of an immigrating ancestor, you usually think of Ellis Island. And why not? About 40 percent of Americans have ancestors who arrived through Ellis Island. So the Ellis Island database of more than 20 million arrival records between 1892 and 1924 can be a juicy find for your research. These records, especially the later ones that have more information, can often be helpful in identifying your ancestor's place of origin.

Of course, not everyone's ancestors came through Ellis Island, even if they arrived during the height of the immigration center's activity. When I couldn't find several Schott and Siewert ancestors at Ellis Island, I was very disappointed. And then I did the research I should have done in the first place and went back to find their Declarations of Intent paperwork, which was required between 1790 and 1952 for anyone who wanted to apply for U.S. citizenship. These showed they'd arrived through Baltimore and Canada rather than through Ellis Island

Also, the Ellis Island indexes were created by volunteers who might have struggled with deciphering the handwriting or with unusual foreign family names. If you don't immediately find your ancestor in the index but know they arrived through New York, it's worth doing a little additional digging because they simply may have been indexed incorrectly.

If your ancestors arrived prior to 1892, they would have entered New York through Castle Garden, which was an earlier immigrant processing center. The Castle Garden site has records from 1820 to 1913, although the majority is prior to 1892.

A useful tool in searching these (and other) sites are on Steve Morse's site, which provides finding aids for the Ellis

Island and Castle Garden sites, a selection of other passenger lists, and a variety of other useful records. Another helpful site for finding resources for passenger lists is Joe Beine's www.germanroots.org/passengers.html site (not just for those with German ancestry).

Genealogybank (www.genealogybank.com)

Genealogybank is a fee-based, but interesting, site with a great collection of U.S. newspapers and obituaries online, as well as a number of other historical documents. The collection of newspapers spans 1690-2010, and even includes some of the small town Dakota newspapers where my family lived (the type of resource that is sometimes hard to find online). The obituaries are priceless to genealogists, and you can also find a number of interesting articles about your ancestors. (I wonder if it was really my grandfather Peter Schott who suffered from a bout of food poisoning in 1921?)

Honorable mention sites

Websites come and go, and each of you will have a very specific research path depending on your ethnic heritage, so it's impossible to include an exhaustive list of good genealogy websites. Cyndi's List is most helpful for digging around to find all the sites most useful for your specific search. But there are a few additional sites worth mentioning:

- **Allen County Public Library**
  (www.genealogycenter.org): One of the largest
  genealogy collections available.
- **New England Historic Genealogical Society**
  (www.newenglandancestors.com): Most useful if
  you have roots in colonial America, but they have a
  number of other useful records, too.
- **The Federation of Genealogical Societies**
  (www.fgs.org): To help find a genealogical
  organization near you or specific to your ethnic
  heritage.
- **International Genealogy Sleuth**
  (www.progenealogists.com/genealogysleuthi.htm):
  This is a professional genealogy firm, but even if
  you don't want to hire anyone to do research for
  you (after all, who wants to miss out on the fun of
  doing the sleuthing yourself?), the site has a number
  of links to good research resources outside of
  the U.S.
- **Chronicling America**
  (chroniclingamerica.loc.gov/search/titles/): A site
  from the Library of Congress that helps identify
  historic newspapers from your ancestors' local
  areas. Its holdings information may not be totally
  up-to-date though, since it was missing information
  about at least one Dakotas-based German-language
  paper that I've used for my research.

- **OnlineNewspapers.com**
  (www.onlinenewspapers.com): A site to help you
  find out if a newspaper useful to your research is
  available online.
- **Black Sea German Research Community**
  (www.blackseagr.org): If you share my heritage of
  ethnic Germans who lived in the Black Sea area of
  Imperial Russia, this website has a growing database
  of family trees and lots of resources available for
  researching this ethnic group. Full disclosure—it
  was started and is run by myself and some of my
  best genealogy buddies.

◆   ◆   ◆

Moving Beyond Online Resources

We would all like to find our ancestors with a couple clicks of
a mouse on a laptop. And with an increasing number of
genealogy records online, it seems like we should all be able to
find our ancestors while sitting comfortably in our own living
rooms.

But I have yet to meet a researcher who has been able to find
their family roots relying only on online sources. At some point
in your search, you'll need to dig into records in archives,
libraries, or county courthouses to find your ancestors. Here's an
overview of some of the key resources you'll need to get familiar
with to research your family.

Birth records

There are a number of different types of documents that can be included in the category of birth records, including:

- Church birth records, usually available from the FHL or from a church archive, sometimes from the actual church.
- Civil birth records, available from state or county vital records offices (in the U.S.) or national civil records agencies.
- Birth certificates and baptismal certificates, which you may find in a family member's attic or closet. A step-cousin of mine found my mother's and grandmother's beautifully decorated baptismal certificates in my step-aunt's attic and rescued them from oblivion (a.k.a. my step-aunt's garbage).

Birth records document the date and location of your ancestors' births. They also usually show the parents' names (or at least the father's name), which helps you find the previous generation. Some birth records also show the child's godparents, which can be useful in unraveling family relationships since the godparents were usually relatives. In at least one case I've seen, the godparents from out of town provided a clue to the mother's maiden name and her birthplace.

Marriage records

These include church marriage records, civil marriage records, and marriage certificates. At minimum, a marriage record will include the bride and groom's names and the date and location of the marriage. But marriage records often include the couple's parents' names (or at least the fathers' names), helping you find that previous generation. They may list the town or profession of the groom (as weddings often took place in the bride's hometown). They may give the age of the bride and groom (useful for estimating their birth years) or some information about previous marriages (if the bride/groom is a widow or widower). The marriage record of my 5X great-grandfather Michael Schott in Osthofen led me back a generation to his father, also Michael Schott, from Ober-Gleen, Germany.

Death records

These include church death records, civil death records, and death certificates, as well as obituaries and informal death notices in newspapers. Death records usually include the name of the deceased and date and place of death. They sometimes include the cause of death and the birthplace of the deceased. This is a great clue for research, but remember that the person (usually the spouse or child of the deceased) giving the information may not know the correct location. The death record may also include the birth date of the deceased, or at least their age at death, to help you guesstimate the birth date. Obituaries and other death notices in newspapers often will list surviving family members and include additional biographical information that can help you learn more about the life of the deceased.

Church family books

Some churches also kept family registers that report on family groups—first the mother and father, then children in chronological order. These are very useful because it can sometimes be difficult to be sure you've found all the children in the family or know which ones are associated with which parents if multiple marriages are involved. Family registers list birth, death, marriage, and confirmation dates and locations for each person. These can be really useful if the family moved from another village as it will generally show where the parents were born or married. These records would usually be available in church archives or through the FHL.

Census records

If birth/marriage/death records aren't readily available for your family, census records can be a valuable source of information because they list all family members and their ages, and sometimes the locations where the family lived previously. Some U.S. census records are available online (for privacy reasons, those less than 70 years old are not available), but census records for other countries may not be. To find census records, check civil archives for the country you are interested in, genealogy societies for the area you are searching, or Cyndi's List to find links to these.

Town history books

In the U.S. and Canada, many towns created history books for special town anniversary celebrations. These books often have family histories and include valuable information about family members, dates, and locations as well as family biographies. Towns in Germany often have *Ortsippenbücher* (town lineage books), which give history about the town and may include very detailed family genealogical data. Wherever your ancestral town is located, it's worth trying to locate any books from that town that include specific family information. The FHL has many of these in their collection, or contact a library or town hall in your ancestral town to see if your town has a book with this sort of information.

Chapter Three

Tips for Successful Research

The baptismal font from the church in Ober-Gleen, Germany, where my ancestors were baptized

A Few Helpful Genealogy Tips

You've got the basics now and should be ready to roll with your research by talking to relatives and digging into sources that are available online and in genealogy libraries and archives. But here are a few additional tips on how to approach your research and further ways to discover clues.

Network, network, network!

Hanging out with other genealogists is one of the most effective ways to find those hard-to-find records or little-known bits of history that could be the key to unlocking a family mystery. Join your local genealogy society. Join genealogy groups that relate to your specific family roots. (I'm a member of several groups that specialize in researching ethnic Germans who lived in Eastern Europe.) Join groups and follow relevant pages on Facebook or Google+, or search out genealogy experts on Twitter. These are the people who are most likely to know how to find records that might not be in one of the big online databases.

These groups and contacts will be useful not only in doing your research but may also be helpful in planning your trip to visit your ancestral town. They can help you find tour planners with specialized knowledge for your area or identify contacts at archives you want to visit. Being a member of such a group may even help you find like-minded friends to travel with, which is what happened for me!

Keep an open mind

Spellings change. Don't assume that the way you spell a name now (both family names and locations) is the only way it has ever been spelled. And don't assume that your names were written correctly by every census taker or every church scribe. I've seen my Dickhoff name spelled Dikhoff, Dikhof, Dickhof, and Dikow (and I'm still wondering about any connection with Dikopf and

Dickhaut). My friend Rich has found 14 different spelling variations of his name, Aspenleiter.

Other names have even more variation. I recently discovered that the original spelling of one family name from the Alsace region, "Schack," appears to have started out as the French name, "Jacques," which actually sounds similar though I would never have thought of that variation.

Having an open mind about spelling was also instrumental in my finding the town where my Schott family originated in Germany. A marriage record for Michael Schott said he came from Oberklein, Hessen. Through a series of serendipitous pointers from fellow genealogists, I started investigating Ober-Gleen, Hessen, and found my guy in the church records there. Be creative.

Keep an open mind, too, on things that "everyone" knows. Assumptions like "Back in those days, Catholics never married Lutherans," or "Christians never married Jews," or "Everyone in that village came from a certain location," or "The first son is always named after his paternal grandfather" can lead you in the wrong direction or cause errors in the data you gather. Every family has exceptions, and you may overlook some good clues or get your family information wrong by assuming that what "everyone knows" is true for your family.

Name variations

In addition to spelling variations, keep in mind that names can vary in other ways. Know the ethnic variations for the name you're searching for. John, Johann, Hans, Yiannis, Janos, Ivan, and Giovanni are all variations of the same name. My grandfather was born Johann Peter, but every source in the U.S. shows him as John Peter. Same guy, different country, different ethnic variation of the name.

The website, BehindtheName.com is useful for figuring out the variations you should keep your eyes open for.

Some of the variations that commonly occurred for surnames are:

- Literal translations (the German surname Weber is changed to Weaver, or the French name LeBlanc is changed to White).
- Shortening names (the name Weisspfennig is changed to Weiss). Who knows, if your ancestor was really creative, he may have lengthened his name in some unpredictable way too.
- Try substituting like-sounding letters (the name Bitz could be spelled Pitz, or the name Klein could become Glein).

Be cautious about what you "know" to be true

Sometimes even what you personally absolutely believe to be true isn't. I was completely certain that I knew all about my Uncle Danny. We visited his family every summer. I hung out with my cousins. My mom always talked about her brother. So of course, I never thought to verify any information about him with vital records or church records.

It took another researcher's database for me to find out that his legal name was Wilbert Theodore. At first, I thought that researcher had bad data, until I asked my mom about this. She said, "Oh yes, he hated his real name and wouldn't use it. He just took his nickname from his dad's name. Didn't I ever tell you that?" Uh, no.

Remember what I said about verifying every piece of information against original records? I should have taken my own advice.

Search both backwards and sideways in time

Even if your main interest in genealogy is searching backwards in time to find your many-times great-grandparents and the towns where they lived, it also pays to search "sideways" in time by connecting with distant cousins or researching your direct ancestor's siblings or cousins.

Another branch of the family might have a photo or other documentation that you don't have. In my case, connecting with a third cousin in Montana led me to a letter written two generations previously by her direct ancestor about our mutual great-great-grandparents and their parents. For many years, this letter was the only hard evidence I had of my 3X great-grandparents since the church records from the early years of Germans living in Russia had been destroyed.

Sometimes researching the siblings of your ancestor can help you locate the family. If your direct ancestors were evasive in recording what town they were born in or what ship they traveled on, you can sometimes track down the family by researching a sibling who was more forthcoming with information. For example, my Siewert 3X great-grandfather consistently showed his birthplace only as Poland or Prussia, while his younger brother was a little less tight-lipped and records his birthplace as Plock, Poland. Although I can't just assume that August (my direct ancestor) was born in the same place as younger brother Karl, this at least gives me a starting place within all of Poland to look for records.

And sometimes connecting with distant cousins is just fun. Through genealogy, I got to know my third cousin once removed, Ute, who lives in Germany. We found out we have lots of things in common and became friends in addition to being distant cousins. I've stayed at her place, and we've roamed around Germany. We've road tripped together through the Dakotas (and Iowa and Minnesota) meeting up with cousins. Just recently, I managed to get to Germany for her dad's 80th birthday celebration. Who knew I'd form new international friendships through my search?

Focus on one ancestral line at a time

It's tempting to dive in and research all your grandparents or great-grandparents at once, trying to find out as much as you can about all of them. But I've found it is often better to really concentrate on one line at a time, following the clues and figuring out where to look next. Genealogy can sometimes be a bit of an art, requiring some creativity to solve the intricate puzzle of your roaming ancestors. I've often found myself noodling on some missing data, "Hmm, if this record says they were in this town in 1816, but no record shows them until 1829, where could they have been in the meantime?" and suddenly a new possibility pops in my head to research.

If you're merely trying to accumulate data about all your family lines, your mind goes on overload. It can be difficult to remember what stage your research is at for each family line, which may keep you from having the mental bandwidth to let your creative problem-solving juices flow.

Focusing on one ancestral line at a time also helps keep you organized so you can file all the records you discover (whether actual paper or digital copies) by family line. Sometimes the joy of the discovery overcomes my inner organizer and chaos reigns in my genealogy paperwork. Don't let it happen to you.

Know the history of the area you're researching

Knowing the history of the area where your family lived is helpful in better understanding your ancestors' lives and giving you at least a little insight into their hopes and dreams and fears, even if you don't (as I don't) have any family diaries or personal papers.

But just as important, a good understanding of the history of the area you're researching can provide valuable clues to your genealogy. Understanding the governments in power or the political situation will help you find out what records are available and where they might be. (Alas, I wish everything was conveniently located in Ancestry or the FHL. But many, many records exist outside those vast libraries and databases.)

Understanding the history of specific time periods may also help you judge the accuracy of any data you find. In some cases, stressful situations can lead to inaccurate records—either because your ancestors simply couldn't remember important information in the middle of a war (or other crisis) or needed to hide something (children's ages, the family's religion) to protect the family.

Diving into the history of the region you're researching can also help you find your family. When researching my Klein family, Lutherans who had lived in Hungary, I knew my ancestor Matthias was born in 1769 in a town called Jenk. I assumed that Jenk had to be in Germany because Matthias lived in an area of Hungary that had been settled by German Protestants in the 1780s when he would already have been a teenager. And although there had been earlier waves of German immigration to Hungary, all my sources said that only German Catholics were allowed in the earlier groups of immigrants. I assumed he must have arrived in Hungary with the later wave of Protestant immigrants.

I searched high and low throughout Germany for a town with a similar name with no luck.

Fortunately, I found a history book that didn't just tell the official story but described what actually happened. Officially, the Austrian-Hungarian government only allowed Catholics in the groups that came between 1718 and 1772. In reality, many Protestants were also included among those immigrants. In some cases, they had to convert to Catholicism, and in others, they settled on the estates of religiously tolerant landowners.

Once I expanded my search for Jenk to include Hungary, I found it relatively easily. And I discovered that my Klein family had arrived in Hungary two generations earlier than I'd expected—probably among the first to make the journey.

I would never have located those two generations without deepening my knowledge of the history of Germans-to-Hungary migration.

Be Creative

Be willing to go beyond traditional genealogical sources. In researching her French-Canadian family, my friend Jackie discovered that one of her relatives had been the executive assistant to Edsel Ford (son of Henry Ford and president of the Ford Motor Company in the 1920s through early '40s). This relative had even been named the executor of Ford's estate. By writing the Ford company, my friend obtained extensive oral history information about her ancestor from the company's 50th anniversary publication.

A car company is hardly a traditional source of genealogical information, but being creative paid off for my friend.

♦ ♦ ♦

Finding Those Hard-to-Find Ancestral Towns

So far, we've focused on the strategies and resources that every genealogist uses to research their family roots. But, of course, your special interest is in finding the locations your ancestors came from so you can walk in their footsteps. For those of us in North America, "jumping the pond" to figure out where our families lived previously can be the most difficult part of our search. Official documents like censuses and citizenship papers allowed our ancestors to be vague about the details of their birthplaces—adequate for the official purposes of the time, but very frustrating for us as researchers. Here are a few ideas to find the birthplaces of your elusive ancestors.

Obituaries and death notices

Death can be very helpful in finding the specific town and location names for your ancestors. Obituaries, informal death notices in newspapers, and even gravestones can be a great source of information. Even if great-grandpa didn't feel the need to tell the census taker anything more than "England" or "Ohio," he probably told his children or grandchildren stories about where he came from, and they are the ones who filled out the death certificate or wrote the obituary. Of course, that can also lead to misunderstandings. My mother grew up in the town of Lehr and always talked about Lehr as her hometown. It wasn't until I started doing research that I realized that she'd actually been born in the neighboring town of Kulm, which she confirmed for me. I was able to make sure my mother's obituary was correct, but I only knew the right information because of my genealogy research. If I'd written it based on what she'd told me all my life, I would have listed the wrong town.

Family papers

Not everyone is lucky enough to inherit an attic full, or even a handful, of treasured family documents. But if you're one of the lucky ones, go through these with a fine-tooth comb to see what clues you can find. Family letters, wills, wedding announcements, even photos (which may have location clues written on the back or names of neighbors that might provide clues) may help you narrow down your search for your family's place of origin.

My friend Jackie's French-Canadian great-grandfather deserted his wife, leaving behind neither support for his young children nor clues to his family heritage. But among her grandmother's papers, Jackie discovered a 1923 letter from a nun in Wisconsin who happened to be her grandmother's cousin. The letter contained some additional family information about the brother of Jackie's great-grandfather who was the nun's father. More importantly, it gave Jackie a new branch of the family to research, which might provide some clues to finding her elusive ancestor's family origins and place of birth.

Local sources

Does the town where your family lived have a historical society or publish any history books of the town? Was your ancestor a business person or leader in town government who might have had biographical information included in the local newspaper? In many towns, even events like having an out-of-town visitor might have been newsworthy enough to get your ancestor mentioned.

Was your ancestor a leader in a local church that might have archive materials, such as church meeting minutes or publications? If you don't know which church your ancestor went to, use the census and city directories to locate churches near their home. Contact the churches to see what records or publications might be available to verify whether your ancestors attended there.

Network with other researchers familiar with the region you're researching as they might be aware of hard-to-locate resources. In the Dakotas, where my family comes from, there were a couple of German-language newspapers (the Dakota Freie Presse and the Staats-Anzeiger) that published letters submitted by their readers. People from villages in Bessarabia, Ukraine, would commonly write to their own family in the Dakotas and include messages like, "Please let my old friend Peter Schott know that his mother passed away in November." When these letters were published in the local German-language newspapers, all people who were originally from that village got to hear a little bit about home. A source like this can also help you locate your family's origin.

Fellow genealogists, local libraries, and historical societies may all help you find sources unique to your area. They also can help you identify which resources are available online and which you need to access physical or microfilm copies at a library or archive.

Sibling rivalry

If your direct ancestors were too tight-lipped to give away their birthplace, try researching their siblings. And cousins. And aunts and uncles—any family member you can track down. One of them must have mentioned their town to someone, so it will show up in their obituary or another record, providing you with a clue to follow up on your own ancestor. This is a good time to track down those distant cousins and see what their branch of the family knows that you can't find.

Neighbors forever

Well, maybe not forever. But it is true that people often traveled to the same place their neighbors did. Fellow German-Russian researchers have told me that their family's neighbors in the Dakotas in the 1900s were the same families they lived near and intermarried with in Russia in the 1800s, which were the same families they lived near and intermarried with in Poland in the late 1700s, which were the same families they lived near and intermarried with in Germany in the early 1700s.

So if you strike out in researching family members, start looking at their neighbors to see if you can identify where they came from. Families who were close to yours may show up near them in the census records, or you may see significant numbers of intermarriages between your family and theirs. Try the same sources I suggested above (obituaries and local sources) to try to identify these neighbors' hometowns.

In addition, this is a really good way to use online family trees—connecting with researchers with similar interests. If you can find these neighbors' names in an online family tree database (Ancestry, Family Search, or any that are specific to your own area of research), these are generally set up so you can easily contact the researcher interested in that family. That researcher may have discovered some information you haven't about where their family came from.

But be cautious not to assume too much. Just because your family seemed close to another family, you can't assume without further documentation that's where your family is from, too. It's simply one more tool that provides a clue in your search.

Ships' passenger lists

Finding the ship's passenger list for your immigrant ancestor may open an important door to finding out where your ancestor came from and how they journeyed to North America.

During the colonial period and through 1820, passenger records are scarce. Some are available through Ancestry. In addition, the German Roots website (www.germanroots.com/1820.html) has a good bibliography of pre-1820 passenger list resources (not just for those of German heritage).

After 1820, an act of Congress resulted in passenger lists being more consistently recorded. However, until 1906, passenger lists for people entering the U.S. still allowed very vague descriptions of a passenger's place of origin. In 1906, passenger manifests were required to add the name and address of the closest living relative in their country of origin. If you're lucky enough to have ancestors arriving in this later time period, passenger lists might give you the clue you need.

Naturalization records

If your ancestor became a citizen between 1790 and 1952, they had to follow a two-step process: first to declare the intent to become a citizen and then, two to five years later, to actually petition for citizenship. Until 1922, a woman's citizenship status was based on her husband's (she became a citizen when her husband did; and if she married a non-citizen, she lost her citizenship). Until 1940, children's citizenship was based on their father's status.

Although the Declaration of Intent and Petition for Naturalization forms left our ancestors the option to be vague about their origins ("Ireland" doesn't narrow down your search much, it's a big island), some people were more forthcoming, and you might find some useful information from naturalization records to track back to where your ancestor came from.

Emigration indexes

You generally know where your ancestors ended up, but if they weren't cooperative enough to record where they came from before that, an emigration index might help. (Emigration is where your ancestor came from. Immigration is where your ancestor went to. My great-grandfather Daniel Netz emigrated from Ukraine. He immigrated to North Dakota.)

In places where residents had to get permission to leave, such as Württemberg, Germany, in the 1800s, there are often civic records of those who emigrated. If you can narrow down the possible locations they might have come from, you can search a bit more efficiently. Knowing that my ancestors came from Germany enables me to skip Australian or Irish emigration indexes. But if I can figure out that they came from the state of Württemberg or Rheinland-Pfalz, that narrows down my search even further to a more concentrated set of indexes.

Search Cyndi's List or Ancestry for online emigration lists. In addition, some are available primarily in book format—check the FHL or civil archives of the locality for which you are searching.

Military records

Enlistment records can give you a pointer to your ancestor's place of birth, even if it is located overseas. The most frequently searched records are those associated with a specific war or military conflict (WWI, WWII, etc.). In addition, the *U.S. Army Register of Enlistments 1798-1914* and the *U.S. Marine Corps Muster Rolls 1798-1940* may have records, and places of birth, for ancestors who served in the military but didn't enlist at the time of a specific conflict. These records are available through the National Archives (www.archives.gov/research/military/) and through Ancestry (www.ancestry.com).

U.S. Citizenship and Immigration Services (USCIS)

Even if your immigrant ancestor never became a citizen, there may be some records with USCIS (www.uscis.gov/historyandgenealogy), such as alien registration forms, that may help you pinpoint where they came from.

Places with multiple names

I've had some special challenges finding the locations of my ancestral towns because my ancestors were ethnic Germans living in what is now Ukraine or Moldova. They had German names for the towns, which carry down today in any stories told by my grandparents or great-grandparents, but these names are not to be found on any current-day map.

If you have a similar challenge searching for your ancestors, be sure to seek out genealogy groups that specialize in your ethnic origins. By using sources from "Germans from Russia" groups, I've been able to find maps and locations of my villages by finding the German names I know cross-referenced with the current-day Ukrainian or Moldovan names.

Check for reference books that may have this sort of cross-index of names. Two I discovered for German research are the *Amtliches Gemeinde- und Ortsnamenverzeichnis der Deutschen Ostgebiete unter fremder Verwaltung* and *Deutsch-fremdsprachiges Ortsnamenverzeichnis*, which show a cross-reference of German village names with the name in the local language.

Another challenge is that your ancestor might have come from a small town. Assuming no one would ever have heard of it, they filled out their paperwork with the name of a larger, more well-known town; just as today, someone who comes from the small town of Puyallup may tell people they're from Seattle, even though it's 40 miles away, because it is more well-known.

And of course, you need to be aware of translations of the place names you're researching. Bavaria and Latvia are Bayern and Lettland in German. Some translations are not at all obvious. For example, the Baltic Sea is Ostsee (literally, East Lake) in German.

Borders change

Yet another challenge in discovering your ancestral town is that the tides of history and national borders ebb and flow, making it difficult to both identify the town based on your ancestors' descriptions and to figure out where to find records. My ancestors lived in an area that belonged to the Turks before they moved there, then became part of Russia, then part of Romania, then Russia again, and is currently partly in Ukraine and partly in Moldova's breakaway republic of Transdniestr. Other ancestors lived in an area that alternated at a dizzying speed between being owned by Poland, Prussia, and Russia. When my ancestors noted their place of birth as Prussia, it doesn't help me narrow in much on their location.

For a really vivid example of how borders changed in Europe from the 1200s to recent times, this video is excellent: http://vimeo.com/89394659.

How does it sound?

In addition to looking at the name of an ancestral town in writing, think about how it sounds. Some letters can sound alike and could be written in different ways, making it difficult to find the village on a map. Some letters that I've had breakthroughs with were *g* and *k*, *d* and *t*, and *b* and *p*. I'd searched for my village of Oberklein/Oberkleen for years until realizing that Ober-Gleen was also a possible spelling.

Chapter Four

Locating Your Ancestral Town

Looking at a map with residents of Benkendorf (Velykomar'yanivka), Ukraine

Searching the Globe

If your ancestral town is nearby or you have specific information about it, this may be as simple as looking at a road map or online map. Even if I hadn't traveled to my parents' birthplace of Kulm every year as a child, it pops up easily on a map of North Dakota. No problem at all finding it.

But when I looked for my grandparents' birthplaces of Hoffnungstal and Gnadenfeld in South Russia, I had a much more difficult time. South Russia is not a specific recognizable geographic region. The area my grandparents knew is currently in the country of Ukraine. However, when I search the term *South Russia* now, the results come back as an area in current-day Russia, far from where these villages actually are.

These were ethnic German villages from the 19th through the mid-20th centuries. Hoffnungstal has been destroyed, although it is still labeled on maps of Ukraine as a ghost town named Nadezhdivka. Gnadenfeld still exists, but is known only by its Ukrainian name of Blagodatnoja. Therefore, looking for either of these villages by their German names on a current map doesn't help me.

Another complication, even after I found information on ethnic German villages in modern-day Ukraine, was that there were multiple villages with the names Hoffnungstal and Gnadenfeld. Gnadenfeld was especially problematic because my grandmother's Gnadenfeld was very small with little information available about it. Another Gnadenfeld, which is much larger, was mentioned in every reference I looked at, but my grandmother's Gnadenfeld was difficult to find.

When there are multiple possibilities for your ancestral town or other uncertainties about its location, be sure to be thorough in your research so you pin down the right one.

Maps

My first instinct these days is to look first at Google Maps. And although this is a great resource, it doesn't reliably find every town. It steadfastly refuses to find my Billigmeier family's hometown of Gräfenhausen, near Annweiler, Germany. (I first located that one using Expedia maps—which apparently no longer exists.) Google Maps also may not recognize a smaller town that has been incorporated into a larger town.

In that case, you'll need to branch out. A great source of links to online maps is on Cyndi's List: www.cyndislist.com/maps. Other great sources are gazetteers (geographical dictionaries) or atlases. These can generally be found in genealogy libraries (such as your local Family History Center) or local libraries near where your ancestors lived. Historical maps that date from the time your ancestors lived there can provide state and county boundaries and may help you locate the nearest church or office where vital records were kept.

There are also online gazetteers. Ancestry has a number of gazetteers online (at least some of which are available without a subscription). Search the card catalog under "Maps, Atlases & Gazetteers." An especially good one for Germany that is available here is the Meyers Gazetteer. Another great gazetteer I use for locations in Germany is gov.genealogy.net/index.jsp.

Genealogy organizations

Genealogy organizations focusing on your ethnic background or geographic area can be a great source of information. Being a member of an organization that focuses on ethnic Germans in Russia helped me find the locations of Gnadenfeld and Hoffnungstal. This organization had a number of reference books, maps, webpages, and knowledgeable people who helped me figure out the correct locations of these villages. Joining an organization on Scottish heritage led my friend Jane to detailed information about the clan her family came from.

Finding a website about ethnic Germans in Hungary and participating in the Listserv for that group was the key to finding out that Jenk was really Gyönk and where it is located. Networking with genealogy researchers who know about your area can be one of the best ways to find your village.

♦ ♦ ♦

Checking the Location

If you have multiple possibilities for your ancestral town or there is any uncertainty about the location you think you've identified, you'll want to confirm you have the right town before planning a trip there. The most certain way to do this is to find birth, marriage, or death records for your ancestor in that town. But if that's not possible, there are other ways to confirm the location.

Even though I couldn't find my grandmother's birth record, I had a pretty good idea which of the multiple villages called Gnadenfeld was her hometown. I knew that most of the people in the area of North Dakota where my grandmother lived had come from an area of South Russia called Bessarabia, so the Gnadenfeld in Bessarabia was most likely my ancestral town. I was able to confirm this by finding a book on Gnadenfeld, Bessarabia, that listed my great-grandparents as founders of the village.

The best ways to confirm your location are:

- Birth, marriage or death records. Church records are usually the best source.

- Other information that is specific to the town that might list the residents, such as town histories, census lists, tax lists, etc.

- The name of your village may contain a reference that will help you. Frankfurt am Main and Frankfurt an der Oder are two very different places. The reference to the river they are near (the Main or the Oder) helps distinguish them.

- Knowing some of the history about these places may help. I knew my grandmother lived in an area settled by people from Bessarabia. I also knew that she was Protestant. So the Gnadenfeld in Bessarabia, which was a Protestant (Lutheran) village, was much more likely to be her birthplace than the Gnadenfeld in the Taurien area that had been settled by Mennonites.

- Sometimes looking at town information and not finding your ancestor's name is a clue. I searched through many records for Oberkleen, Germany, where I was sure my Schott family was from, but could not find any Schotts. Not finding them on the tax lists encouraged me to search further (because surely, if *any* lists would be complete, it would be the lists used to collect taxes!), and I found them in Ober-Gleen, Germany.

Chapter Five

Planning Your Trip

A street in Osthofen, Germany

How to Prepare for a Successful Trip

Now that you've located your ancestral town, it's time to start planning the details of your trip. You'll need to make the standard travel plans any traveler makes—airlines, rental cars, Eurail passes, and hotels. But you'll also need to make plans specific to visiting your ancestral town.

By spending more time researching and making contacts before you leave, you'll have a better chance of seeing more places specific to your interests while you're there. How much time you spend depends on how important it is for you to visit specific locations in your ancestral town and how comfortable you are making the contacts.

Different ways to plan your trip

You can plan your trip using a standard tour group, a specialty tour group, or by making your own arrangements independently. Each has pros and cons.

A standard tour group is the easiest travel experience to plan since the tour agent will generally make all the arrangements. This is the best option if you don't have time or aren't comfortable making your own arrangements. Although this method is unlikely to give you the opportunity to visit a specific ancestral town, you'll get a good sense of the country or culture without worrying about travel planning or navigating in an unfamiliar place.

Some tour agencies specialize in heritage tours to locations specific to family history and genealogy interests. Using one of these agencies to visit your ancestral town can give you the benefit of having someone else do most of the work to organize the trip.

A tour operator might be able to customize a tour just for you and your family (although this could be more expensive depending on the size of your group), or you may travel with a group that shares similar interests. In that case, you need to be prepared that the travel time will be split between your own ancestral towns and that of others in the group.

Traveling independently gives you the most flexibility if you are comfortable taking on the travel planning yourself. But this option also takes the most time in advance.

I've used all these methods at one time or another. It's important to plan a trip that is comfortable for you and your group, balancing how much work you want to do with how many specific locations you will be able to visit.

Things to consider when making travel plans

Finding your comfort level

If you're merely driving across the state to visit your parent's hometown for the first time, you probably have a pretty good idea how to get there and find your way around. If you're a seasoned traveler, even if you're going to a new location, you may also feel pretty comfortable navigating your way and making your own travel plans.

But if you're going to another country for the first time or to a culture very different from your own, or if you haven't had much experience traveling, you may want to have someone else do all or most of the trip planning as well as guiding you while you're there.

You'll also want to think about your travel companion(s) and their comfort level with the travel arrangements. Even if you're such a seasoned traveler that you're comfortable arriving in a country and making arrangements on the fly, that might be too stressful for your elderly mother or cautious brother traveling with you.

Prepare for local conditions

It's a good idea to get an understanding of local conditions at your destination so unpleasant surprises don't negatively influence your trip. When my cousin-in-law visited her father's hometown in Cambodia, her parents warned her about the lack of electricity, lack of running water, and squat toilets in a shed. Knowing this in advance helped my cousin-in-law mentally prepare, so she could take the basic accommodations in stride. Her advance knowledge paved the way and allowed her to enjoy the family connections she was making rather than being distracted by the living conditions.

What are your trip deal breakers?

Before you start planning, it's good to understand what is most important to experience on your trip. What are your "deal breakers," the places or experiences that, if you missed them, would leave you feeling you'd wasted your trip?

Is it the church where your grandparents were married? A specific house or cemetery? Are you happy with whatever you might see? Or do you just want to get a glimpse of the culture? Are you a genealogist hoping to do research while on your travels? Are you trying to meet distant relatives?

How specific your goals are will help determine the type of travel planning that is best for you.

If your main goal is to experience the culture, your preparation will be similar to any other traveler, ranging from making the travel arrangements to reading up on the general history and sights of the area you're visiting.

If you want to stroll through your ancestor's town, you'll at least need to locate where it is and find out how to get there. You may also want to do a little background reading about that town.

If you have some very specific places you want to see in your ancestral town (e.g., your great-grandparents' home, a cemetery in a hard-to-find location), you'll want to do more work ahead of time. Is there a family member who can take you there or give you directions to find the place on your own? Is there a visitors' bureau? In a smaller town, you might write or e-mail the town mayor or town council, the pastor of a church, or the person in charge of a local museum.

There's also research you can do on your own. This can range from looking up addresses and searching online for a location, to looking up old Bureau of Land Management (BLM) township maps, to looking at plat maps of foreign villages. If your ancestors lived in a city, like New York or Stockholm, it can actually be more problematic to find specific houses or buildings (which may have been redeveloped over the years) so more digging is needed.

On a recent visit to North Dakota, I decided to visit the country cemetery where my great-grandfather and great-great-grandmother are buried. I'd been there before but always with one of my local relatives who knew their way around the gravel section line roads. This time, a friend and I ventured out with the BLM township maps as our main guide. This meant veering off the county highway onto gravel roads, hoping we'd read the map right as we traveled through acres and acres of farmland with no other landmarks in sight.

Fortunately, due to a national emergency preparedness initiative, there are now "city-style" rural road signs at each section line crossing. This made it a bit easier for a city girl like me to find a country cemetery that is miles from any town. And we only went down one wrong road! (It seemed like a good idea at the time to take the shortest route back to the main county road, but it was a mud pit.)

The one disappointment of this excursion was that I hadn't prepared a bit more. When I got home, I realized the country school both of my parents had taught at used to be almost directly across the gravel road from this cemetery. Even though I know the schoolhouse is gone, it would have been fun to look more closely at the spot where it had been located.

On a trip to Ukraine, I went to much more elaborate lengths to find the "house" where my ancestors had lived, even though the house no longer exists. After the ethnic

German villagers (including my grandfather's brothers' families) left in 1940, a military base on an overlooking hill had used the empty houses for target practice. All had been destroyed.

Even though I knew this when I went to Ukraine, I still came prepared with a map of the village. Although the houses were gone, regularly spaced steppe-grass-covered mounds were clearly the overgrown rubble of each of the homes. My group drove to the north end of the village and then carefully counted the mounds to reach the one I thought might have been the home of my great-great-grandparents.

Inexact, I know. Even one extra out-building in one family's farmyard could have thrown our count off. And there was really no way to know if I was in the right spot. But as I posed for a photo on that grass-covered mound, then searched the area for a shard of the original red tile roof, I felt as though I'd made a tiny connection with my family's past.

Making your travel plans

If you've decided that ease of planning is most important to you and you have a minimum number of specific places you want to visit, you'll probably opt for a package tour. Try local travel agencies, search the Internet, and ask friends and family members for package recommendations that will best meet your needs.

If you've decided to travel independently, you have some decisions to make about travel arrangements and what you want to see in your ancestral town. We'll cover that later in this chapter.

If you've decided to use a specialty travel group, you'll need to locate the best one for your location. Read on!

Finding a specialty travel group

A specialty or heritage tour group is your best bet if you want the convenience of someone else organizing your trip but want to be sure to visit your specific ancestral town. The most reliable way to find a specialty tour group that will meet your needs is to network with other genealogists specific to your area of interest, perhaps through joining a genealogy organization, through websites, or through Facebook and Google+ groups and pages.

My family background is very specific—I'm a German from Russia. My ancestors were ethnically German, but from the late 1700s to the early 1800s, they all immigrated to villages in Imperial Russia, in a region that is now Ukraine and Moldova. In addition to helping me with my research, joining a Germans from Russia genealogy organization also made me aware of organized trips to Ukraine with tour operators who had excellent local contacts with people in my ancestral towns.

In addition to finding the tour organization I used for one trip to Ukraine, I connected with other like-minded people interested in this type of travel. So when I did go on that trip, I went with 12 colleagues rather than 12 strangers. We may or may not have been compatible if we were randomly thrown together simply through common travel schedules.

For another trip to Ukraine, I traveled on a semi-independently planned trip with three friends I met in this genealogy organization. With this small group, we could set our own travel plans and even change them midway through the trip when we wanted more time somewhere.

If you're looking for a specialty tour group, check out my website www.carolynschott.com/ancestry-travel for my up-to-date list on travel resources for planning your trip. If you don't find an option there, a few other suggestions are:

- Subscribe to publications that relate to your family's background. These specialty tour agencies usually advertise there.

- Search the Internet using key words such as specialty travel genealogy, heritage travel, genealogy travel, family history travel, genealogical vacation, or ancestral travel.

Of course, you'll want to do some due diligence and check out the travel firm's credentials and reputation. You may ask to speak with past travelers before sending in a deposit.

Making your own travel arrangements

If you're willing to take on responsibility for the trip planning, traveling independently of a tour group gives yo great flexibility. It gives you the most control over you schedule and the places you visit. It often allows you to make more personal connections with people in the place you're visiting, rather than just with the other people in your group. The appendix of this book has a number of travel resource suggestions to help you with your travel planning.

One of my best experiences was traveling to Gyönk, Hungary, ancestral home of my Klein family. I spent the day with Janos, the town mayor (who also ran the local German heritage museum), and was invited to lunch with him and his wife. Not only did I get a tour of the town and cemetery, but I also got a glimpse into the daily lives of the people living in Gyönk today through my conversations with Janos, his wife, and the local pastor.

Although the visit started off with some formality—the town mayor escorting a visiting American—that formality was soon discarded when Janos got into my rental car and discovered how badly I drove a stick shift. (This was the only rental option in Budapest, and my only experience driving a stick shift before this trip was a half hour in a Seattle parking lot as a friend tried to show me the basics.)

Hesitantly at first, Janos began to coach me on when to shift, which opened the door to a conversation about ⁓⁓⁓ⁿᵗoms in Hungary versus the U.S. A little laughter he joined in) at my ineptness shifted the versation from formal tour to At the end of the day, Janos insisted I return to his home and share a Hungarian aperitif with him and his wife before driving back to Budapest.

While the arrangements for this trip were a bit complicated to figure out on my own, it became a much richer and more personal visit than I could have experienced with any tour group. As I left Gyönk, I waved good-bye with genuine regret, having spent time with some great people I never would have met, or laughed with, or shared a meal with, otherwise.

Appointments

If you want to visit archives or libraries to do research, you'll definitely want to find out the hours they're open, their policies about visitors, and if an appointment is necessary to use their materials, microfilm readers, or computers.

Even if you're going to an ancestral town just to look around and don't have a specific agenda, making contact in advance with someone local can often enhance your visit. Churches, which most people want to see, are often locked during the week. If you want to visit a specific home or meet new relatives, advance contact is even more important. Even the most hospitable people may find it disconcerting to have a stranger show up on their doorstep saying, "Hi, we're related," or "Hi, my family used to live in your house." In small towns, contact the local town hall, the mayor, a local museum, or the church pastor.

Opening communication before you arrive is a great way to make some personal connections. I first contacted Marie-Luise because the pastor in one of my ancestral towns recommended her due to her interest in local history. We'd been in contact by e-mail, and I paid her to do some research for me. So when I was traveling to Germany, I definitely wanted to meet her.

In person, we really hit it off. She showed me around several villages in the area, explaining the complex history of how these different villages had belonged to different German princes. I got to see the inside of the church in my village and meet the pastor's wife. We visited a little-known local museum and met with an elderly woman who had a lot of local history information. We even sat in Marie-Luise's living room, looking through a 16th-century tax book that the local archive had entrusted to her.

On my next visit, I stayed with Marie-Luise rather than in a hotel, and she looked positively insulted when I tried to pay her for some additional research she'd done for me. "We are friends now; I will not charge you!"

In a way, there wasn't much to see in this ancestral town—no cemeteries or houses that I knew to be connected to my family. But with Marie-Luise as my guide, I got a great overview of the history of the area and met some interesting people I would never have met by going to a museum or simply walking through a cemetery. And I made a friend!

Of course, sometimes an unplanned visit does work. An older woman and her two granddaughters showed up at my house in Seattle one Saturday. The woman had lived in my house when she was a child, the family (who all lived elsewhere now) happened to be in Seattle visiting friends, and she wanted her young granddaughters to see the house where she'd grown up.

I decided she didn't look like an ax murderer, so I invited her in. She gave me a tour of my own home, describing the changes that had been made over the years. She and her sister had shared what was now my bedroom, and she drew a line in the air to show where they'd had a strip of tape to stake out their own halves of the room.

I could tell she enjoyed seeing her old home again; her granddaughters got to see a bit of their family's history, and I learned some things about my own home I'd never known.

Language and translators

If you're traveling outside of North America as a tourist, you can usually get along fine knowing English and being willing to try a little impromptu sign language. English has become a world language and most countries' tourist facilities (hotels, transportation companies) are staffed with at least some English speakers. Even if you get into a momentary situation where no one around you speaks English, you can generally point or pantomime what you need.

But if you travel outside of tourist areas as you visit small ancestral towns or archives, the chance of finding English speakers goes down rapidly. If you want to know specifics about a village's history or about using a microfilm reader, pantomiming is unlikely to work well. In that case, if you don't speak the local language yourself, you may want to find out how to hire a translator or ask in advance if someone is available who speaks English.

If you don't speak the language and don't have a translator, consider using Google Translate (if you have Internet access) or a translation app on your phone (most convenient if it doesn't rely on the Internet). Another great translation tool is the book, *Point it: Traveller's Language Kit*, which is a picture dictionary that allows you to communicate by pointing at pictures.

On a recent trip to ancestral towns in Poland, I followed a suggestion from my cousin Justin, who has also done a lot of travel to ancestral places. I created a page of simple sentences, then used Google Translate to create Polish versions. (My name is Carolyn. My German ancestors lived in this village about 1800. Is there an old German cemetery?) It worked wonderfully in one village, and the people I talked to really engaged in reading it and pointing me in the direction of the cemetery. (It worked less well in the other village, but I think I just caught people in the middle of their work day and they didn't have time to deal with a random American wandering around their town.)

Another option would be to create questions along with multiple choice answers for them to point at. The question "Who lived in this house before you?" might have multiple choice answers like: a) my parents and grandparents; b) I bought it from someone I know; c) I bought it from a stranger; d) I don't know. This method can provide more information than if they just launch into a long, detailed explanation in a language you don't understand.

I haven't found standard foreign language phrase books and apps to be very useful. These usually focus on tourist-related words and phrases, rather than those useful when visiting an ancestral town. Knowing how to say "Where can I buy a ticket?" is less useful than, "My ancestors lived here in the 18th century, and I would like to see the inside of your house."

◆ ◆ ◆

Do Your Genealogy Ahead of Time

If your main goal is to visit your ancestral town (versus a research-focused trip), you'll definitely want to do your genealogy ahead of time rather than expect that you will find out information in your town. Most church records no longer reside in the original towns and are now in church archives, so you'll be disappointed if you have high expectations for unlocking new clues. And although you may meet distant cousins with all the genealogical answers you've been seeking, you can't count on that happening.

When I went to Ober-Gleen, Germany, I knew it had been the birthplace of my 5X-great-grandfather Michael Schott. Although he moved away from the village, he left behind his sister, Anna Elisabetha, whose married surname was Jacobi. When I asked around, it turned out that there was a large Jacobi family still in the village. Unfortunately, they knew little about their genealogy back to the 1600s, and I hadn't researched Anna Elisabetha's descendants. I probably had distant cousins that I could have met if I'd done my homework.

Come prepared

You'll want to have non-Internet-dependent (paper or phone app) family history information with you so that it's easily accessible when you meet a potential distant cousin or want to verify that the gravestone you're looking at is really your ancestor.

It's also useful to bring along any village maps or historic photos you might have of the village to show to locals so they can help you locate important buildings (your ancestor's home or the site of a church or town hall that may have been torn down or re-purposed).

And then there are the basic things, such as being sure to have extra batteries for your camera or a notepad to write down information. These things can seem small but can lead to huge disappointment if you don't have the right tools at the moment when you finally find that gravestone or talk to your grandmother's former next-door neighbor who knows more about your family than your own family does.

Doing research during your travels

If you want to do genealogical research in your family's ancestral town (or a nearby library or archive), you'll definitely want to do some pre-planning. You'll want to make some contacts in the place where you're going before you leave on your trip, and you'll want to be sure to come prepared with your specific genealogy data. Some archives or libraries require an appointment to use microfilm readers or to ensure that someone who can help you is there.

When planning a research trip to Germany, I discovered the Hessen state archive had an online catalog. Not only did this help me develop a list in advance of the documents that I wanted to review at the archive, but I discovered these documents were in the Wiesbaden branch archive rather than the (more obvious) Darmstadt main archive. This was critical to my trip planning; otherwise, I would have ended up in the wrong city to do my research. This also helped me make the best use of my time at the archive. I could focus on looking at the documents rather than spending time figuring out which ones were likely to help me. Therefore, doing a little advance planning made this archive visit much more productive than if I'd just shown up on the doorstep.

If you plan to do research while on your trip, it's good to have an idea of what you're looking for and to bring along whatever information you need from your own records at home.

♦ ♦ ♦

A Few Last Tips

Here are a few miscellaneous tips for your ancestral town travels that I've learned over the years:

- Ask anyone and everyone for help. Sometimes the grumpy old men (or even the drunk old men!) and the little old ladies eyeing you suspiciously while sitting on a bench snapping peas in their garden can turn out to be your most helpful sources.
- Find the mayor or town hall or any other local administration to find out more about the history of the village. They may direct you to a museum or school or local history enthusiast.
- When you're in your ancestral town, don't be shy. Engage in conversations. It can be a delightful way to get to know the locals and maybe find out information about your family. I thoroughly enjoyed the debate in the town of Freudental (Mirnoye, Ukraine) about whether a specific house had previously belonged to Germans. We started talking with the owner of the house who had recently purchased it and wasn't sure. More neighbors joined in to offer their opinions, and the conversation moved out into

the street and down to another neighbor's home.
Someone suggested that yet another person would know,
and the whole conversation group drifted down the street
to find out his pronouncement. I'm not sure that we ever
decided, but it was great fun engaging the neighborhood
in the lively debate.

- If you meet someone (or see something) with one of your
  family names, introduce yourself and ask questions. It
  could lead to some serendipitous new discoveries. Of
  course, that doesn't happen every time. I tried so hard to
  get a conversation going with a winemaker at a family
  winery in Osthofen. I love wine, and the family name was
  Müller, which was one of my family names from that
  village. I know Müller is a common name, but after all,
  my people were also from that village. Yet I couldn't get
  more than a grunt or "uh huh" from him. Oh well.

- Bring back a piece of your village. Of course, don't do
  anything illegal or bring back anything Customs would
  frown on when you're trying to re-enter your home
  country. But a stone or small amount of dirt or pressed
  flower can make your memory of the visit very tangible
  when you're back home.

- Sleep in your ancestral village if you can. My cousin
  Justin, who visited the village of Neudorf (Karmanova,
  Moldova) said, "I know it's not always easy, but I loved
  knowing that I had slept in Neudorf 70 years after the last
  Ehresmann had left. *Loved* it."

- Be aware of places where your family traveled through, even if they didn't spend enough time there for you to consider it an ancestral town. That gives you the opportunity to plan a genealogy-related side trip if you happen to be nearby. While vacationing in London, my cousin took a day trip to Southampton, England, as his family had traveled to America on a ship that stopped there. The local library helped him find the newspaper announcement about the ship's arrival and departure times, giving him all sorts of interesting details about local weather and events. Although the stop in Southampton was not a major part of his family's story, it provided a few more details and a little color to the dry facts he'd previously known about their voyage to America.

- Avoid drinking games with the locals. Especially if your village is located in a country where drinking could have its own Olympics team. Not speaking from personal experience on this one, but from a trusted, fellow ancestral-town-travel enthusiast.

- As preparation for your travel to your ancestral town, or as a substitute while you're saving up for that dream trip, consider a virtual visit by zooming in on the town using Google Earth (www.google.com/earth/) or finding photos of the town by going to maps.google.com, hovering over "Satellite" and clicking on photos.

Chapter Six

The Trip of a Lifetime

The memorial to German settlers in Hoffnungstal (Nadezhdiva), Ukraine

Planning and Chance May Create a Memorable Trip

When things go right, your visit to your ancestral town lets you experience a little bit of the life your ancestors experienced. For me, the most memorable trips are those where I make personal connections, so the trip becomes more about the people rather than just the places.

Traditions live on

On my first trip to Ukraine, I visited Hoffnungstal, the village where my grandfather was born. I knew the village had been destroyed, so I wouldn't be able to see much.

Still, I walked on the hill where the cemetery had been. Though all the stones were gone, I knew that several generations of my family lay somewhere beneath my feet. I looked down into the valley that had once held a thriving village of several thousand people and imagined I was seeing it as my great-great-grandparents had when they first arrived there. I walked on the faint track worn through the steppe grasses and tried to see the street as it had been in my grandfather's time—wide and bordered with neatly whitewashed stone walls.

Later that evening, we were staying at the home of Micha and Mascha, a Ukrainian couple who lived in a village a couple miles away from Hoffnungstal. Mascha and her sister had made strudels (a kind of dumpling) for us, just like my mother had made. We didn't have a common language and had to rely on Serge, our guide, to translate for us. Despite this, the warmth of laughing and toasting together, and eating the foods I'd grown up with, gave me a sense of connection. Though my grandfather's village was gone, the traditions of food, hospitality, and gathering around a table in laughter remained unchanged.

From strangers to colleagues to neighbors

Bob, one of my genealogy colleagues, visited his ancestral town in Ukraine and the house where his grandfather had lived. As he got to know the family living there, a single woman supporting her daughter and her mother, he realized how difficult it was to support a family in the Ukrainian economy. With the unemployment rate at 70 percent in the nearby city of Mykolaiv, Valya had been unable to find a job. Her mother, Olga, had previously worked on one of the collective farms, but did not receive a pension.

Bob looked for a way he could help this family that was more caring than simply handing them money, and then flying back to the U.S. and forgetting them.

It took a few years of thought and planning, but Bob eventually started a specialized tour service for those of German-Russian background to visit their ancestral towns in Ukraine. Valya became the tour organizer and guide; then later her daughter, Karolina, took over the business. As chance would have it, the tour business became the setting for romance. Valya married a man on one of the tours and moved to the same state where Bob and his family live.

Bob's visit to his ancestral town led to a long-term friendship between Bob and Valya's families, the business has helped provide financial stability for Valya's family in Ukraine, and the two families now live less than an hour apart in South Dakota. Talk about an impact he won't forget!

A sense of connection

Visiting my parents' hometowns in North Dakota has led to some important personal connections for me.

When I visited my mom's hometown of Lehr for its 100th anniversary celebration, I met my stepcousin Lynette. I suppose we'd met when we were kids, but she was one of the "big" kids, seven years older than me, and so we'd never known each other well. As we've grown closer, we've discovered that we're not only step first cousins on my mom's side of the family, we're also third cousins on my dad's side. When Lynette's aunt was going to throw out a box of old stuff from her attic, Lynette looked at it and recognized the photos and documents were from my family. Knowing of my interest in genealogy, she decided to take it home to give to me rather than let her aunt throw it away.

Without her intervention, my grandmother and mother's baptismal certificates, plus a number of family photos, would have been thrown in the trash. I was so thankful to have made that connection and gotten to know Lynette.

I also feel a real sense of connection when visiting my dad's hometown of Kulm. When I was a child, we went there almost every year on vacation, so visiting Kulm was not a particularly new or long-awaited experience for me. But a recent visit as an adult reminded me of my connection to this small town.

My cousin, who lives there, and I were walking down the street. My cousin stopped to talk with a couple of men, introduced me as his cousin, and added, "This is Harry's daughter." The men's nods and murmurs of assent showed they understood clearly where I fit in the family.

Although my dad had grown up in this town in the 1920s and '30s, he'd moved to Seattle almost 60 years before. We'd only visited a few days each summer after that, then my dad died about 30 years ago. Yet these men clearly knew who my dad was, how he fit into the family, and therefore how I fit.

I grew up in Seattle where a lot of people don't know their own cousins, let alone the cousins of friends and neighbors. This small encounter made me feel part of the thread of life in this small town because of my family connections.

Learning your own personal history

The visit my cousin-in-law Meatra made to her father's hometown in Cambodia helped her better understand her father's personality and ambitions. Family history information has been impossible to find because most records were destroyed during the Pol Pot regime (1970s) or lost when her family had to flee the country. Some of her family members were killed during that time, and so even the oral history and family stories have been lost.

But visiting her father's hometown, meeting her aunts and uncles for the first time, visiting the school her father attended, and seeing the rural village and bamboo houses on stilts all gave her a greater insight into her father's determination to build a new life for his family.

◆ ◆ ◆

Sometimes a Disaster,
Sometimes an Adventure

Traveling can be unpredictable, even when you've been a careful planner. Most problems are simply annoying, although on occasion a problem may have more serious consequences (health, passport problems). But if you're going on a long-planned-for and hoped-for trip to an ancestral town, anything that interferes can be emotionally disappointing, too.

There are common sense ways of protecting yourself from specific problems. Travel insurance can help cover the cost of nonrefundable tickets if you need to cancel your trip or a natural disaster causes major delays. Travel medical insurance can help cover you if a health issue occurs. Checking references or ratings for an unknown travel agent, airline, or hotel can give you peace of mind that it is legitimate.

But the best way to protect yourself from the most common types of travel mishaps, such as flight delays or weather problems, is simply to have the attitude that you'll make the best of whatever happens. As a bonus, making the best of any situation can lead you to unexpected, positive experiences.

Problems visiting your ancestral town

Beyond common travel issues, there are some problems unique to visiting ancestral towns. For example, you can get incorrect information and go to the wrong town. On my first attempt to locate my ancestral town in Germany, one of the genealogy reference books I used showed my family had come from Ludwigsburg, Baden-Württemberg. Given the excellent reputation of this book and lack of time before I left on my trip, I assumed the information was correct.

Ludwigsburg is a beautiful town of around 90,000 people with a small, ornate castle in the middle of town. It's fairly well-known in Germany but not known to most American tourists. I had no specific information about my family living in this town, so I couldn't look for a church or a house to visit. It was a large enough town that even finding a cemetery was difficult. So I just walked through the downtown square looking around.

I enjoyed the town as a tourist but really didn't feel any sense of familiarity or attachment. In fact, I was frustrated because I arrived at lunchtime and couldn't find any restaurants other than the Wienerwald (fast food) and a lot of German cafés, which have only ice cream and coffee drinks. Even though I knew it was silly, I kept thinking, "The way my family eats, any town without restaurants can't be the home of my ancestors!"

Although my reasoning was shaky, my conclusion turned out to be correct. When I returned home and did more research, I found out my family wasn't from Ludwigsburg but rather from a town called Osthofen. (I suspect they received their emigration papers in Ludwigsburg, and that's what caused the mistake in the reference book, but I have no actual proof of this.)

It was disappointing that I hadn't seen my actual ancestral town. But I enjoyed visiting a place most American tourists don't see. I enjoyed visiting the castle. I tolerated eating at the Wienerwald, and the ice cream was pretty good, too. And on a subsequent trip to Germany, I managed to get to Osthofen. Even though Ludwigsburg wasn't my ancestral town after all, rather than consider it a wasted trip, I chose to make the most of my visit as a tourist in an unfamiliar spot.

Extra preparation can prevent these types of disappointments. When I was in Ukraine, our guide had the town of Gnadental (Dolinowka in Ukrainian) on our list of villages to visit but not Gnadenfeld (Blagodatnoja), where my grandmother was born. Gnadental is a larger, older ethnic German village in this area. Gnadenfeld is a small village that was founded much later. Serge, our guide, had never had anyone ask to go to Gnadenfeld, so had assumed I was mistaken and I really meant Gnadental.

But this time I'd done my homework. I knew the correct village, knew where it was on the map, knew for sure it wasn't Gnadental, and was able to get us to make a course correction and visit the village where my family had actually come from.

Of course, even when you find the right village, the visit can sometimes be disappointing. When my friend Elli visited the village of Sangerowka, Ukraine, where her mother had grown up, she expected the cemetery would still be standing and the village would still exist. Her cousin had visited 10 years before and had described all this to her.

Instead, she found the gravestones removed from the cemetery, plowed over to plant more crops. Only a couple of houses were still standing; most were small piles of rubble with the wind swirling clouds of dust between them. The effects of time and abandonment had taken their toll.

My friend Rich thought he was heading for a similar disappointment. He'd hoped to spend a night in the house where his father had grown up in Speier (Pischani Brid in Ukrainian). Before his trip, his guide Karolina had tried to arrange this, but the current homeowner insisted she didn't want anything to do with Rich. (Perhaps fearful he would try to stake some claim to the house?) Fortunately, once Rich was there in person, he was able to convince Nellie that he was no threat. She relented and allowed Rich and his wife to at least walk through the home and take photos.

Sometimes a bad tour guide can mess up your plans. On my first visit to Freudental (Mirnoye), our guide took us to the middle of the village and announced, "This is Freudental. The cemetery is gone; the church is gone; the school they're using now wasn't the one used in German times." Then she looked at me expectantly, apparently assuming I would say, "Okay, let's go then."

But I wasn't satisfied with two minutes in the village where my great-great-grandparents had met and married and where my great-grandparents had been born. Fortunately, our driver, Peter, and I had become buddies (despite his lack of English and my lack of Ukrainian). I ignored the guide, showed Peter the map I had of the village, and he started asking people on the street what was there.

With Peter's help (and the guide's grudging translation), I got to see the cemetery (mostly gone except a few headstones), the site of the original church, and the ruins of one of the community buildings. Sometimes you have to take matters into your own hands and use whatever allies you can find to make sure you can see what you want.

Health and injuries

Of course, sometimes more serious problems come up, like accidents or health issues or volcanic eruptions that cause flight cancellations. (I'm not kidding about the volcanic eruption—I was flying out of Germany the day Iceland's Eyjafjallajökull volcano erupted. It made for a long travel day.) Such unexpected events could cause you to cancel or cut short a trip, missing the ancestral towns you'd hoped to visit. There's very little you can do at this point other than be philosophical and know you'll have to plan another trip. And hopefully you've done your trip preparations well enough that you have either the resources or insurance to cover yourself.

But some situations can be salvaged. Having the attitude you're going to make the best of whatever comes up can take you a long way toward making the situation work and minimizing the disappointment.

On my first trip to Ukraine to visit ancestral towns, I was already in Europe when the 9/11 terrorist attack occurred in 2001. My friends were supposed to fly from the U.S. on September 13, but all air traffic in and out of the U.S. had been stopped. While our travel plans were among the most minor casualties of that tragic day, it did turn our arrangements upside down. We needed to quickly decide whether we were going to continue the trip or not; and if we did, how to change our plans.

We decided to go ahead and scrambled to change our flight, guide, and hotel reservations. Many of our friends told us we were crazy to be traveling out of the country during that period of uncertainty after the attack.

But traveling outside the U.S. in the wake of this terrorist attack actually gave our trip more meaning. I'll never forget the elderly man in Kassel (Komarivka, Ukraine). Although age had left him infirm, physically and sometimes mentally, I'll never forget him standing in his home in rural Ukraine—no running water, three generations living in a one-room house—with tears flowing down his cheeks as he talked about the victims in New York's World Trade Center.

On my most recent trip to Ukraine to visit ancestral towns, I had an inconvenient and painful accident. I was in Bosnia prior to meeting up with my friends and I broke my foot by stumbling over the two-inch-high threshold of my hotel door.

This could easily have ruined my trip. I was given a "walking cast" (actually a bit of plaster around my heel wrapped with flimsy gauze) that was too fragile for me to tromp around cemeteries and muddy, rutted roads in rural Ukraine. I was in pain and in tears and ready to give up, change my ticket, and head home.

But my friends and I had planned this trip for a long time, so it was disappointing to give up on it. Once the painkillers kicked in, I started to think about how to make the trip work and came up with an elaborate scheme. I called a friend in Seattle who had a key to my house. She picked up the orthopedic boot I'd saved from a previous foot injury and FedExed it to my hotel in Vienna (where I was meeting my Ukraine travel friends). The boot arrived at the hotel in the afternoon. I arrived at the hotel early evening. I snipped off the cast with a pair of desk scissors and replaced it with the boot. The next morning, I met my friends at the airport ready to do as much of the trip as I could.

My biggest challenge was visiting Hoffnungstal, a village that was very important to me. On my last visit, I'd discovered that the memorial stone, commemorating the existence of the village, had been vandalized. But one of my German cousins had told me a new one had been built, and I wanted to see it. Also, my genealogy mentor Dale, who helped me start my own research and who had planned to be on this trip with us, passed away several months before. His family had also come from this village, and we'd planned a short silent memorial to him.

Our guide, Karolina, had a map that showed a dotted-line outline of a village, indicating this was a ghost town because it had been destroyed. We drove along the rutted dirt track, with no signs of life—not even sheep—for miles. Karolina kept asking me, "Does this look familiar?" because she'd never been there before. Finally, I recognized the contour of the land dropping toward the valley.

Just as I was pointing to a group of trees on a hill that matched my memory, the road dipped downward, and the van came to a halt. An enormous mud puddle lay across the road, with no way to know how deep it was. The fields were too uneven on either side to drive around. Vova, our driver, just shook his head and said a few words to Karolina. Even without knowing Ukrainian, I knew he was saying we couldn't go any farther.

I looked up the hill. Not an especially long walk, but the track was rocky and uneven. I'd broken my foot less than a week earlier, and the only thing protecting it was the orthopedic boot. The boot wasn't particularly comfortable to walk in, so hiking up this trail seemed like a bad idea. Everyone in the van looked at me. I was the only one with an interest in this village, so it was up to me whether we stayed or left.

It seemed crazy to hike up that hill, but even crazier to come halfway around the world, be so close, and not actually make it to this spot I'd so wanted to see. I just said, "Let's go," as I crawled out of the van. Inna grabbed my arm to help me, and several of my friends hovered nearby as we slowly hiked up the track toward the cemetery.

I had to pass up walking through the ruins of the town (impossibly far away in the valley below)—at least for this trip. But I made it to the cemetery, saw the memorial, and we let feathers fly in the wind to honor our friend Dale.

Was I especially courageous? Or foolhardy? No, I was just determined to make the best of the situation, even with a broken foot. Experiencing an ancestral town is worth a little inconvenience and hardship.

Chapter Seven

What's Next?

Singing with my hostess, Marina, in Kyiv, Ukraine

Further Exploring Your Family History

Maybe you've just started to get interested in your family genealogy. Maybe you've done a little research, but are trying to figure out the next steps to find an elusive ancestor. Maybe you've been to your parents' hometowns, but are now ready to visit an ancestral town in another country.

Wherever you are on your journey into family history, I hope this book has encouraged you to take it to the next level.

Sparking an interest

My first visit to my ancestral towns—my parents' hometowns—happened at about the age of nine months when my family made a road trip from Seattle to North Dakota. We repeated that trip almost every summer as I grew up.

The vast expanses of prairie that my parents experienced in their childhood; the magic of a small town and being able to walk out my aunt's back door, through her backyard, and be on Main Street; the rhythm of life based around the seasons and the three-times-per-day blare of the town's siren (noon, 6 p.m., and 10 p.m.) were so different from my own daily existence in Seattle that it opened up a whole new world for me. I'm sure it was these annual trips to my parents' hometowns that whet my appetite to see other places my family had lived.

As I learned more about my family history, my goals for what I wanted to see both expanded and became more narrowly focused. I needed to get involved in genealogical research of my family to find out more details about who they were, where they'd lived, and what they'd experienced. I didn't do my research with a specific plan to visit my ancestral towns, mostly just wanting a better understanding of my heritage and where I'd come from.

When I started visiting ancestral towns, of course, I loved learning more about where my family had lived and getting a glimpse of their lives there. But I found that I enjoyed getting to know the local people I met, even if they weren't directly connected to my family history, just as much as thinking about my ancestors. The people I've gotten to know and the places I've visited in my ancestral town travels have come to hold a special place in my heart.

Taking it to the next level

Where do you go from here? With everything you've learned, you should be ready—to start your research, tear down some genealogy brick walls, or plan your travel to places where your family has roots.

Connecting with your family's history and visiting the places where they once lived can help you get a deeper sense of who you are and where you come from. Your journey may not always lead exactly where you plan. You may encounter unexpected people or events along the way. Embracing those serendipitous experiences becomes a part of your journey, a part of the family history you are creating as you search.

◆　◆　◆

Appendix

Tools and Travel Resources

Genealogical Standards of Proof

As you dig into archives and old records, you might have to evaluate if you've found enough information to be sure you have identified your ancestor and the right ancestral town. The Board for Certification of Genealogists has developed the Genealogical Proof Standard. Because we can't all find the perfect set of records to document our ancestors' lives, the purpose of this standard is to give guidelines on what is "good enough" in your research.

Even if you're not a professional genealogist (most of us aren't), these standards are useful to keep in mind for your own genealogy. They can help you decide when it's safe to conclude you have the right information or have pulled together enough information to reach an informed conclusion. If you've covered the following five elements, you have done your best to reach a solid conclusion.

1. Reasonably exhaustive search

This is a formal way of saying "leave no stone unturned." Have you been thorough in looking at—and searching for—a wide range of sources (church records, civil records, land records, census records, etc.)? Are your sources high quality? (That is, not just talking to Great-Aunt Mathilda or looking in a database of undocumented data.)

The goal is to ensure that you haven't missed an important source, leading to new evidence coming up later that disproves the conclusion you've made about your ancestor.

2. Complete and accurate citation of sources

It's crucial to use high-quality, reliable sources and to document those sources. This way, if you, or your great-grandchildren after you, ever want to go back and verify what you've found, any of you can follow the same trail and come to the same conclusion. This is basic in science—an experiment should be repeatable by someone other than the original scientist to be credible. If another genealogist can follow your trail, you've probably come to the right conclusion.

3. Analysis and correlation of the collected information

Almost all of us have been thrilled at some time by reading a murder mystery—seeing the clues unfold and then shaking our heads as we think, "I would never have guessed it was him!" when the detective cleverly puts all the clues together and determines the murderer.

This is where you look at all the information you've gathered, look at the sources you have and how reliable they are, and draw your conclusions about your ancestor based on the evidence you've uncovered. It's important that all your evidence supports your conclusions and that you're not ignoring any facts simply because they don't seem to fit your interpretation. If that's the case, there may be an even more interesting answer. You'll just have to keep digging to find it.

4. Resolution of conflicting evidence

Often, we have conflicting evidence about where and when an ancestor was born, married, died, or lived. One ancestor of mine was born in 1816 in the village of Neudorf, according to multiple reliable sources, mostly church records. Yet a census of Neudorf taken in 1816 did not show the family in that village. Conflicting data, both from reliable sources.

For years, I had a question mark by this piece of data. I couldn't resolve the conflict because all of my sources were equally reliable. Another researcher finally helped me out; he'd found a copy of an addendum census in another archive that showed my family and one or two others arrived in the village in the fall, after the original census was taken in the spring. Finally, my conflicting data was resolved with a reasonable explanation, and I deleted the question mark.

5. Soundly reasoned, coherently written conclusion

Basically, this is your final conclusion, based on all the data you've gathered and after resolving any conflicts. As a hobby genealogist, it may seem like overkill to write out your conclusion. But I've found it to be immensely helpful to document in the notes section of my genealogy software the evidence I used to reach the conclusion I did. That helps me retrace my steps (with thousands of ancestors in my genealogy database, I can't always remember why I decided to believe one date or location over another). I also have my family tree online for others to access, so it will help them better understand the data as they incorporate it into their own family tree.

Interview Guide

When interviewing a family member about family history, your basic strategy is to get them talking and remembering. It's often best to start off with open-ended questions such as, "Tell me about your parents and what you remember about them," which (hopefully) will open a floodgate of anecdotes and information.

But if the person you're interviewing is a bit more reticent or gives you brief answers that don't provide much information, it can be helpful to have some prepared questions to draw them out.

Below is a list of more than 100 questions to help prompt your conversation. I wouldn't recommend showing your interviewee the long list—they might be terrified! This list is just a tool. Pick and choose the questions most likely to get your interviewee to open up.

At the end of your interview, I suggest asking, "Is there anything I haven't asked about that you'd like to talk about?" I've found the new information that may pop out may be really amazing.

I also would suggest recording your interview to make it feel more like a conversation than an interview in which you're taking detailed notes, which can make the person being interviewed feel self-conscious.

Basic Family Information

Personal information

1. What is your full name? Why did your parents select this name for you? Did you have a nickname?

2. When and where were you born?

3. How did your family come to live there?

4. What do you know about your family surname?

5. Is there a naming tradition in your family, such as always giving the firstborn son the name of his paternal grandfather?

6. What is the full name of your present spouse?

7. When, where, and how did you first meet your present spouse?

8. How long did you know him/her before you got married? What did you do on dates?

9. What was it like when you proposed (or were proposed to)? Where and when did it happen? How did you feel?

10. Where and when did you get married? (Include date, place, church, etc.)

11. Were you married more than once? If so, answer the previous questions about each spouse.

12. When and where did your spouse die?

13. How many children did you have all together?

14. What were their names, birth dates, and birthplaces?

15. Why did you give them the names that you did?

16. Do you remember any advice or comments from your parents or grandparents that had a big impact on how you lived your life?

17. What were the hardest choices you ever had to make?

18. What is the most stressful experience you ever lived through?

19. What is the single most memorable moment of your life?

20. Is there anything you have always wanted to do but haven't?

21. Were you ever mentioned in a newspaper?

22. Where was your first home?

23. In what other homes/places have you lived?

24. What was your profession, and how did you choose it?

25. What was your first job, and what other jobs have you had?

26. If you served in the military, when and where did you serve, and what were your duties? Rank?

27. Were you ever injured in the line of duty?

28. What was your religion growing up? What church, if any, did you attend?

29. What was the religion of your parents and your grandparents?

Parents, grandparents, and other extended family information

30. Who were your parents? Please give full names.

31. Where were they born, and where did they grow up?

32. When and where did your parents die? What do you remember about it?

33. How did they die? Where were they hospitalized and buried?

34. What are the full names of your brothers and sisters?

35. Could you tell me a story or any memory of your brothers and sisters?

36. Where did your spouse's parents live?

37. What do you remember about the death of your spouse's parents?

38. Who were your grandparents? Please give full names.

39. Where were they born, and where did they grow up?

40. Were there other family members living in the same area when you grew up? Who?

41. Who was the oldest relative you remember as a child? What do you remember about them?

42. What stories have come down to you about your parents? Grandparents? More distant ancestors?

43. Are there any stories about famous or infamous relatives in your family?

44. Are there any physical characteristics that run in your family?

45. Do you remember hearing your grandparents describe their lives? What did they say?

46. Do you remember your great-grandparents?

47. Do you have any relatives who live in foreign countries?

48. Do you know which of your ancestors immigrated to America? Do you know where they came from? Have

you heard any stories about how they traveled to America?

49. Do you have any family photos I can look at and make a copy of?

50. Has anyone else in the family ever gathered genealogy information? Who?

Family Events and Daily Life

Questions about daily activities can help you better understand your relatives' lives and the events that most influenced them.

Home

51. What was the house (apartment, farm, etc.) like where you grew up? How many rooms? Bathrooms? Did it have electricity? Indoor plumbing? Telephones? Computers?

52. Were there any special items in the house that you remember?

53. What are your earliest memories of your home?

Personal memories

54. Tell me about your earliest childhood memory.

55. Of all the things you learned from your parents, which do you feel was the most valuable?

56. Tell me about yourself as a young person. What were you like?

57. What accomplishments were you the most proud of?

58. What is the one thing you most want people to remember about you?

59. Do you remember having a favorite nursery rhyme or bedtime story? What was it?

60. What were your favorite toys or games, and what were they like?

61. What kinds of books did you like to read?

62. How old were you when you started dating?

63. Do you remember your first date? Could you tell me something about it?

64. Name a good friend you have known the longest. How many years have you been friends?

65. What kinds of musical instruments have you learned to play?

66. What are your hobbies, or what do you like to do when you're not working?

66. What organizations or groups have you belonged to?

67. Have you ever won any special awards or prizes as an adult? As a child? What were they for?

68. What was the favorite place you ever visited, and what was it like?

69. As a child, what did you want to be when you grew up?

70. What was your favorite job and why?

71. How long did you have to work each day at your job?

72. Did you have any of the childhood diseases?

73. Do you have any health problems that are considered hereditary?

74. Have you ever been the victim of a crime?

75. Have you ever been in a serious accident?

76. Has anyone ever saved your life?

77. How do you feel about the choices you made in school, career, spouse?

78. How did you find out you were going to be a parent for the first time?

79. How did you first hear that you were a grandparent, and how did you feel about it?

80. What advice do you have for your children and grandchildren about being a parent?

81. What advice would you give/did you give to your child or grandchild on his/her wedding day?

Family memories

82. What did your family enjoy doing together?

83. Did you have family chores? What were they? Which was your least favorite?

84. Did you have any pets? If so, what kind and what were their names?

85. Describe a typical family dinner. Did you all eat together as a family? Who did the cooking? What were your favorite foods?

86. How were holidays (birthdays, Christmas, etc.) celebrated in your family? Did your family have special traditions?

87. Have any recipes been passed down to you from family members?

88. Describe the personalities of your family members.

89. Are there any special heirlooms, photos, Bibles, or other memorabilia that have been passed down in your family?

90. Do you remember anything your children did when they were small that really amazed you?

91. How did you feel when the first of your children went to school for the first time?

92. If you had to do it all over again, would you change the way you raised your family?

School

93. What was school like for you as a child? Where did you attend grade school? High school? College?

94. What were your best and worst subjects and why?

95. Who was your favorite teacher, and why was he/she special?

96. Tell me about any school activities and sports you participated in. Did you ever win any awards?

97. Who were your friends when you were growing up?

98. How do your fellow classmates from school remember you best?

99. Did you and your friends have a special hangout where you liked to spend time?

Culture and society

Questions about culture, society, and daily activities can help you better understand the world in which your family member grew up.

100. Do you remember any fads from your youth? Popular hairstyles? Clothes?

101. What were your favorite songs and music?

102. What world events had the most impact on you while you were growing up? Did any of them personally affect your family?

103. How is the world today different from what it was like when you were a child?

104. Do you remember your family discussing world events and politics?

105. What wars have been fought during your lifetime?

106. What were you doing when you heard the news of the Pearl Harbor bombing? Or the assassination of John F Kennedy? Or 9/11?

107. What would you consider the most important inventions during your lifetime?

108. Do you remember the first time you saw or used a television, a car, a refrigerator, a computer, the Internet, a smartphone? (Substitute any others that apply.)

◆ ◆ ◆

Travel Planning Checklist

Any travel requires at least a little bit of planning, even for the most spontaneous adventurers. And of course, some people are planners who like to have their whole trip planned from A to Z. Here's a checklist of items to consider when planning your travels. Some of these apply only to international travel.

- **Itinerary:** Choose your destination and plan your trip itinerary.
- **Passport:** Make sure your passport is up-to-date and valid for at least six months after your trip (an entry requirement for some countries). Make a copy to take with you (and carry it separately from your actual passport to make it easy to replace if stolen) and a copy to leave at home or with a friend as an additional backup.
- **Visas:** Obtain visas, if needed, for any countries you're visiting.
- **Flight/hotels:** Make any necessary flight and hotel reservations.
- **Rail pass:** In many countries, getting around by train can be much simpler (and less expensive) than renting a car. In most cases, you'll buy train tickets at local stations during your travels. But if you'll be making extensive use of the train in Europe, for example, it may be worth it to buy a Eurail pass. These must be purchased ahead of time in the U.S. See www.eurail.com. (Note that other destinations also have rail passes, though I personally

have less experience with these. The site,
www.internationalrail.com, shows some of the options.)

- **Rental car:** Make rental car reservations, and check on
insurance. Some credit card companies cover your
insurance when renting a car, but there are lots of fine
print and conditions. (Imagine my surprise when I found
out Visa didn't cover my rental car insurance in the
civilized first world country of Ireland. Too many
American tourists banging into the stone walls while
driving down the left side of narrow Irish roads, I guess.)

- **International drivers' license:** Obtain an international
driver's license if you'll be renting a car. Although I
almost always get one (from my local AAA office), I'll
admit that I've rarely needed it in recent years as many
countries don't require them. Still, if you're not sure, it's
best to be prepared.

- **Money:** Travelers' checks are so 1990s. Many places will
either laugh at you or just stare blankly if you try to use
them. I always carry some cash (generally small amounts
kept in different places), especially to get through the first
24 hours of a trip.

Throughout my travels, I rely on ATMs to get local
currency and then use credit cards for those few big
expenses. Be sure to let your credit card company know
you'll be using your card outside the country to avoid
fraud alerts and having your card shut down.

Also, many countries are now using credit cards with chip and pin technology that aren't used in the U.S. I've only run into a problem once (at an automated kiosk) because my card didn't have the chip, and have generally been able to use my U.S. credit card for hotels and big purchases in stores. But it's something to be aware of so you're not caught short of payment options. The website www.independenttraveler.com has current information about what to consider and updates on current issues regarding obtaining money in other countries.

- **Family research:** Bring along your family research, maps, etc., both in electronic format on your laptop or tablet and a paper backup copy. It also doesn't hurt to have a copy somewhere such as Dropbox (a free cloud-based file hosting service at www.dropbox.com) to make it available in the off chance that your possessions are stolen.

- **Local contacts:** If you've made local contacts or appointments, be sure to have their addresses and phone numbers so you can locate them or contact them if your plans change.

- **Other contacts:** It's helpful to make sure you have a list of emergency contacts (friends, your credit card company, travel insurance company, etc.) with you.

- **Travel insurance:** Buy travel insurance. I never used to bother with this, and then I broke my foot while traveling and started to think about the level of medical care in some places I've been and what I would have done if it had been a more serious accident. I've used World Nomads (www.worldnomads.com) because it was recommended by Lonely Planet, but I'm sure there are others.

- **Cell phone:** Check with your cellular carrier about global roaming plans for the countries where you'll be traveling, and ask them about rates for voice, texting, and data. If you have an "unlocked" cell phone, a cheaper alternative when traveling overseas is to buy a local SIM card. A local SIM card means you'll have a different phone number each place you go, but it can save you money if you use your cell phone a lot.

  Also, be very cautious about data usage, which can cause your phone bill to skyrocket. Talk to your cellular carrier about how to turn off and manage your data usage while traveling. The ins and outs of international cell phone usage change all the time, but www.independenttraveler.com usually has current information about the best options.

- **Prescriptions, glasses, etc.:** Be sure to have everything critical for your comfort and well-being with you (not in checked baggage), including a copy of any vital prescriptions.

- **Vaccinations:** Get any needed vaccinations. (Consult a travel health doctor or see wwwnc.cdc.gov/travel/destinations/list to determine what you need.)

- **Guidebook:** A good guidebook is worth its weight in gold.
- **Duct tape:** Don't laugh. I can't tell you how many times I've found a good use for duct tape. Well, yes I can tell you. See my blog: www.carolynschott.com/travel-accessories/duct-tape-dont-leave-home-without-it. My most creative use of duct tape was to hold my friend's toilet tank together in her flat in Moldova.

❖ ❖ ❖

Guidebooks and General Travel Resources

Online travel resources

Doing an Internet search for the name of the place you're going will likely yield more websites than you can look at. Try combining the place name with *tourism* or *history* or *archives* or *museum* to get a more focused set of results for what you'd like to see in your ancestral town or the area.

Each of the guidebook series listed below also has a website with travel information, blogs, and discussion boards. These discussion boards are especially useful because travelers using a guidebook you like will probably have a similar outlook on travel as you do, making their feedback especially reliable.

Some other websites that give feedback from actual travelers are www.tripadvisor.com, www.virtualtourist.com, and www.yahoo.com/travel. One caution about relying on feedback from these sites is that you don't know if the person commenting has interests or tastes similar to your own. I read one review that was very critical of an Eastern European hotel. From the comments, it was apparent this person expected American-style accommodations, which was unrealistic in that region unless you stay at a Hilton or Sheraton or one of the other big name hotels. I knew this; the reviewer apparently didn't. (They complained about the very things I thought added to the charm of the place.) Since their expectations differed from mine, their comments were not useful to me.

Another site to explore is www.wikitravel.org. Similar in concept to Wikipedia, the information is provided by people with an interest in a specific geographical area. It lists sights, hotels, restaurants, transportation, and Internet cafés.

Transportation

You'll need to arrange transportation from home to your main destination. If that's an airline, you can book your travel either online or through a traditional travel agent. Online travel options are constantly changing, but some good websites for flights are www.kayak.com, www.expedia.com, and www.orbitz.com. I've also had good luck with www.whichbudget.com for flights within Europe (although this site also covers travel to other destinations).

You'll also need to arrange transportation within your destination area to your ancestral town. Depending on the local situation and your comfort level, this may be a rental car, train, bus, boat, or taxi. I usually like to rent a car because it gives me the most flexibility. But that may not make sense if it's a destination where you're not comfortable driving. In that case, I'd probably use the train, public transportation like a bus or marshrutka (minibus that is common in Eastern Europe), or, in some cases, hire a car and driver. (That sounds extravagant, but it is actually a very practical alternative in some places.)

To help you plan your trip, up-to-date schedule information for trains, long-distance buses, and boats is available online or through a travel guidebook. This can help you decide on routes and transportation alternatives. For example, I didn't want to rent a car and drive in Croatia and Bosnia, but when I saw the complexity of the connections, I realized a car was my only option without completely changing my itinerary.

Also consider local conditions. Even though I'm a reasonably independent traveler, I've always hired a driver in Ukraine and Moldova because the roads in rural areas are unbelievably bad, signposts are nonexistent, and border crossings in Moldova are problematic. There are often local police who stop you to get a bribe (which happened twice on my last trip there). Fortunately, with Vova, our knowledgeable driver, at the wheel, this was handled with no problem and actually became part of the adventure. My cousin Justin has also successfully used marshrutkas to travel to ancestral towns in Ukraine and Moldova.

Hotels

You may want to reserve rooms in advance or you may just play it by ear. (Personally, I like to have a hotel reservation when I fly into a country or if I arrive somewhere late at night, even if for the rest of the trip I plan to be more spontaneous.) I've had good luck with www.booking.com for hotel reservations. A guidebook can also provide suggestions for you.

If you're traveling during a high tourist season, you may want to reserve in advance to prevent the uncertainty of having to hunt for a room or the dubious adventure of ending up in a fleabag place. On one spontaneously decided overnight stay in London, I ended up in a hotel in which I suspect the other guests were paying by the hour. I couldn't get out of there fast enough the next morning.

I generally like to be as spontaneous as possible. But on one trip, I realized with all the appointments I'd made, I was tied to a schedule that didn't allow for much spontaneity. So it made sense to book everything in advance rather than spend time looking for a hotel in each location. If you're only going to be somewhere a short time, you may not want to waste your precious time there searching for a hotel.

Guidebooks

Many great travel guidebooks are available that can give you detailed information about planning the basic logistics of your trip, including flights, rental cars, and hotels. I would advise picking a guidebook that fits your personality and travel style, then follow the suggestions there. Each guidebook series targets different types of travelers, with different budgets and travel expectations.

Of course, if you're traveling to an ancestral town, there's a good chance you'll be off the beaten path in a location that no guidebooks mention. However, you may prefer to find a hotel in a nearby larger town covered by a guidebook and visit your ancestral town and other sights from that base.

My own favorite series for European travel is the Rick Steves' guidebooks. The philosophy of this series is to "travel like a temporary local." They are written in a lively and humorous way. They do a great job of highlighting the most interesting sights (and are blunt about telling you when a famous sight is not actually that interesting). They also have very good insights about the country and its culture and people, as well as practical information on everything from transportation to where to do laundry or find an Internet café.

I think Rick does a good job of covering a wide range of accommodation choices, from very nice hotels to hostels, with a focus on clean midrange hotels. (Although one college-age traveler I talked to in Slovenia told me his suggestions were all too upscale and expensive for her, despite his hostel listings.)

In Europe, I also often use the Michelin Guides. The familiar green-colored guide gives thorough listings of any possible sites in almost every location in that country. The red guide gives hotel and restaurant recommendations with equal thoroughness. Although they focus on higher end accommodations (I usually find myself choosing the hotels listed as low end in their books), I like them because they cover so many small locations so thoroughly. This is useful when looking for a place to stay in towns not covered by traditional guidebooks, which tend to focus on tourist areas.

Guidebooks are available that cover Europe, Asia, North and South America, Australia, Africa, the Caribbean, etc. Some of the major guidebook series are Fodor's, Frommer's, Lonely Planet, Bradt, Let's Go, Access, and Rough Guides. Each of these has its own style and focus, which vary from targeting upscale travelers to backpackers; from popular destinations to remote ones; from classic sights (the Eiffel Tower in Paris) to lesser known attractions (the Museum of Oil in Ploieşti, Romania).

The Fodor's and Frommer's series both tend to focus on more upscale travel. Their hotel suggestions are generally more expensive and Americanized; the sights they review are more traditional. Frommer's has some good information on family-friendly hotels and sights.

Lonely Planet guidebooks cover low- to moderate-priced accommodations and are thorough and well-researched with lots of maps. They're informal, but informative, in their descriptions, and can be blunt, for example, when something is a rip-off. These are my favorites when traveling places the Rick Steves' books don't cover.

Rough Guides guidebooks use contemporary language and include good, detailed information, although I know people who have used this series and report that information is not always easy to find quickly. These guidebooks focus on low budget travel and less mainstream sightseeing options. The Let's Go guidebooks have a similar focus to Rough Guides.

The Bradt guidebooks cover more unusual destinations and are champions of sustainable travel, with a decent amount of practical information and a range of accommodation choices.

The Access guidebooks focus on cities and organize their information by neighborhood. This series may not be useful to you unless you're staying in a city while doing day trips to your ancestral towns.

Look for the guidebook that best suits your style of travel because hotel, transportation, and even sightseeing recommendations are geared toward its typical audience.

For the U.S., I usually travel with the AAA guidebooks, free with my AAA membership. They do a good job of thoroughly covering accommodations, even in smaller towns, which can be useful on a family history trip. Some of the travel guide series mentioned above also cover the U.S. and Canada.

Many of these guidebooks are available in e-book formats, such as Kindle, Sony Reader, or iPhone. This can give you the option of taking several with you without carrying multiple bulky guidebooks. However, all e-book readers may not show maps and other illustrations well, so you may want to consider how important those are to you.

❖   ❖   ❖

About the Author

Carolyn Schott has more than 50 years of experience visiting ancestral towns, dating back to her very first road trip to North Dakota to visit her parents' hometowns in North Dakota. She has been researching her family history seriously for more than 17 years (and dabbled a bit before that). She is one of the founders of the Black Sea German Research website, has been on the Board of Directors for the Germans from Russia Heritage Society, and is a member of several other genealogy societies that coordinate research efforts for ethnic Germans in Eastern Europe.

Carolyn has visited many of her own ancestral towns in North Dakota, Germany, Ukraine, Hungary, Moldova, and Poland. She blogs about her travels to ancestral towns (and other travels whenever she can slip away from her day job as a grant writer for an international nonprofit organization). Visit her at www.carolynschott.com

CPSIA information can be obtained
at www.ICGtesting.com
Printed in the USA
LVOW12s1731130416

483457LV00002B/288/P

101

Simple Seafood

Recipes

by Pam and Bill Collins

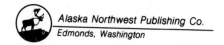
Alaska Northwest Publishing Co.
Edmonds, Washington

Library of Congress Cataloging in Publication Data

Collins, Pam, 1953-
  101 simple seafood recipes.

  Includes index.
    1. Cookery (Fish) 2. Cookery (Shellfish)
  3. Seafood. I. Collins, Bill, 1952-   . II. Title.
  III. Title: One hundred one simple seafood recipes.
  IV. Title: One hundred and one simple seafood recipes.
  V. Title: Simple seafood recipes.
  TX747.C74 1987   641.6′92   87-14491

Alaska Northwest Publishing Company
130 Second Avenue South
Edmonds, Washington 98020

Printed in U.S.A.